A TIDE THAT SINGS

Sister Agnes, of the diocese of Aberdeen and Orkney, was born in Nottingham and spent her early years in a small mining town, the daughter of a fitter's mate and his handicapped wife. At an early age she was influenced by the life of Francis of Assisi, and also by the more spartan spirit of the Celtic Church. An introduction to Scotland added a touch of magic. All these, and the tragic early death of a much-loved mother, drew her inevitably towards the fulfilment of the religious life, which she now follows as a solitary on the remote island of Fetlar in Shetland.

With line drawings by the author

SISTER AGNES

A Tide that Sings

TRIANGLE

First published 1988
Triangle
SPCK
Holy Trinity Church
Marylebone Road
London NW1 4DU

British Library Cataloguing in Publication Data

Agnes, *Sister*
  A tide that sings.
  1. Christian life —— 1960-
  I. Title
  248.4   BV4501.2

  ISBN 0-281-04339-6

Photoset by Inforum Ltd, Portsmouth
Reproduced, printed and bound in Great Britain by
Hazell Watson & Viney Limited
Member of BPCC plc
Aylesbury Bucks

To our Lady Mother of Christ
and in memory of my parents
Elsie and Bernard

Acknowledgement

I am deeply indebted to Mrs Dorothy Jamieson of Fetlar for her encouragement, patient and most constructive criticism, typing out of the manuscript and in short, for teaching me to write.

Contents

Foreword *by the Rev. Prebendary T. Derwent Davies*

1   Childhood *1*
2   Schooldays *9*
3   Nanny *19*
4   Scotland *29*
5   Sorrow *39*
6   Greenwoods *52*
7   Joycroft *60*
8   The Convent *70*
9   Mothering Sunday *79*
10 A Harbour *85*
11 Iona *94*
12 The End of an Era *102*
13 Fetlar *109*
14 Blessings *116*
15 Miracles *123*
16 Home *131*

Notes *144*

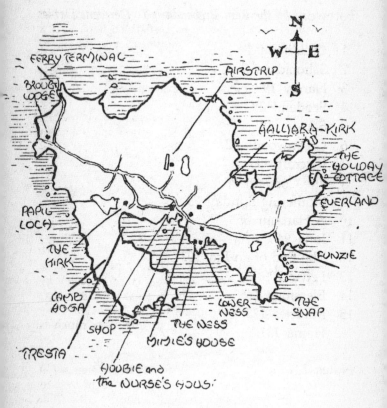

The Island of Fetlar

Foreword

The author of this fascinating book, as well as having the ear of a musician and the eye of an artist, has the soul of a dedicated Christian whose consuming passion is to know and do the will of God.

Her ear is well tuned in to the tide that sings, a tide that comes near to her door and whose music gladdens her heart day by day.

Her eye observes and feasts upon those rare species of birds for which Fetlar is well known to all British ornithologists – from the lovely snowy owl to the black guillemot (symbol of the Shetland Bird Club). There are virtually no trees on Fetlar, one of the three most northerly islands of Shetland, but in spite of this northerly location there are over two hundred species of flowers for the eye to enjoy.

For the Franciscan soul there is much more to enjoy. Although this little island, of no more than fifteen square miles in size, with its frequent dark days and fierce North Sea gales, is as different as anything could possibly be from the warm, gentle and sunny clime of Assisi, one cannot doubt that St Francis would nevertheless love Fetlar and its people, its birds and its flowers as much as he loved their Italian counterparts.

Nor can one doubt that he smiles tenderly upon Sister Agnes who is so thoroughly imbued with his spiritual ideals as she worships, works and witnesses in and around her little croft, and among the kindly Fetlar folk for whom this nun (probably the one and only to arrive there since the Reformation) must have been, at first, as odd a sight as God's own 'little funny man' himself.

Like her patron, she has chosen to embrace a life of poverty. The cupboards of Assisi and Fetlar have much in common! But the joy of this nun, like that of her master, is in inverse proportion to the quantity of her possessions.

The name Fetlar, (which, rather ironically, means 'fat land') is derived from the old Norse language. It is one of the most remote islands of the Shetland group, with a population of fewer than a hundred.

Not one of them is far from the 'tide that sings', and now that Sister Agnes is among them, bringing the music of Christian discipleship in fresh – yet ancient – ways, they realise that nuns as well as tides are good at singing. They have certainly taken her to their hearts. They see her as a reflection of God's light – and in a part of the world where for considerable periods of the year light is a scarce commodity extra illumination is very precious. Not surprisingly, the Fetlanders are saying of Sister Agnes, 'We need her here.' And this after a mere three-year relationship.

Her ordered life of constant prayer and extremely hard work – cultivating the croft land, repairing roofs, mending fences, operating a primitive printing press, feeding cats and birds and caring for lambs, visiting the sick, teaching the Faith to children – is all within the context of the recitation of the daily offices faithfully performed. This is all offered to God in a spirit of love and has the effect of building up the 'spiritual fatness' of the land.

My ten-day stay on Fetlar in the summer of 1986 was an unforgettable experience. I followed in distinguished footsteps, hot on the heels of the then Primus of the Scottish Episcopal Church who had given Sister Agnes his blessing and commended her to the prayers of his people. It was thrilling to find ecumenism (one of the great facts of this century) flourishing in Fetlar. The minister of the kirk has welcomed Sister most warmly and shown her much kindness. He is pleased that she is able to reside on the island whereas he cannot, and their friendly relations are strengthened by the fact that on the two Sundays in the month when he conducts service in the kirk Sister Agnes is a member of his congregation. The Roman Catholic priest who lives in Lerwick has also been kind and helpful – as have a number of his flock.

Sister Agnes's own parish priest, whose parochial responsibility covers the whole of Shetland (with his vicarage on the Mainland), visits her at regular intervals and celebrates Holy Communion in her little oratory – with the blessing of his Diocesan, the Bishop of Aberdeen, within whose jurisdiction (in the city of Aberdeen itself) there is a religious community which faithfully prays for 'Fetlar and its nun'.

With such support from so many quarters, Sister Agnes is wonderfully fortified and it is clear that God is blessing her endeavours and using her in many lovely ways.

I hope the publication of this little book, so sensitively written, will further enlarge her circle of praying friends, and if God so wills, incline the heart of some young woman to join her in witnessing to those Christian values which, amid the cacophony of weird noises in our modern society, represent divine music.

The tide is indeed singing – for those who have ears to hear.

T. DERWENT DAVIES

1 Childhood

It was dark, and I lay in the huge double bed which I shared at that point of my life with my mother; and felt my small heart, for I was no more than an infant, hammering like the rain on the window pane, and beating as it had never done before. It was the first, and one of the few times that I have ever felt afraid, and so terrified was I, that I dared not move, not even to bury my head under the bedclothes. Instead I stared transfixed and frozen with fright at the horror on top of the wardrobe. I could see, as though I were suspended above them, four horrible, grotesque little gnome-like men, sitting on stools at a round table, smoking long clay pipes and playing a game of cards. Their ugliness chilled me to the bone. I wanted my mother. Wordlessly I called and called again, until in sheer desperation and panic, I flung out an arm to see if she were there. She was, and instantly the phantoms of the night vanished, dissolved into nothingness, and I slept.

Only twice during my childhood did I experience such fear, and on each occasion it served to induce some dim awareness in me that in my perfect world there was something bad.

The second time I must have been almost seven, and again it happened in the dark of the night. It was that same hideous nightmare, although this time my sister, a toddler, lay sprawled in great abandonment in the three-quarter bed beside me and was too young, and too deeply asleep, to care. I must not, though, go off at a tangent, for a tale with too many deflections may never get told. Instead I must return to the point where the story began.

The wind howled and the rain beat ceaselessly through

1

the night on to the windows of a row of dreary pit houses in a small Nottinghamshire mining village. The year was 1944 and my mother and I were living temporarily in two rooms of one of them, my grandmother's home, until the war ended and my father, a soldier, returned from abroad.

A close and lasting bond was knit between my mother and me during those early years, for we were each a reminder to the other, of him who was absent.

Both parents were simple working class folk and content to be so. At an early age my mother had been afflicted with polio, and remained for the whole of her comparatively short life, a cripple. As a young woman she had been warned for her own sake not to marry, and if she did, most certainly not to bear children. However, she wanted a family and took the risk. With four and a half years between us Carole and I were brought into the world, and were soon to learn that the greatest characteristic of our mother was that loving sacrifice she always so willingly bore, not only in the great issues of life, but also in every lowly and humble day-to-day event, for those she loved. She taught me of love, sacrifice and laughter from the moment I was able to learn, and still I am influenced by the example of this woman who was my mother.

The first shadow of the cross to fall across our lives as a small family became apparent to me on a grey wintry day before my fifth Christmas. Both my parents looked blanched and weary, were hardly aware of my presence, and stole around the house preoccupied and strangely silent. Carole, eight months old, and deathly still in her cot was, I feared, the reason for their distraction. They gazed at her from moment to moment, then helplessly at each other.

'The vicar should be here soon,' each intermittently stated, both keyed up and straining to hear his first rap on the door. All seemed to depend upon this man, 'the

2

vicar', and when he did arrive he was eagerly welcomed and taken at once to the source of their perplexity. He was very old. I knew that because his hair was white, and as he stood looking down at the bundle of a baby who was my sister, I was inclined to think he might even be God. His voice was gentle, and I, being a child, and probably because I was a child, knew with a surge of happiness in my unnoticed corner, that Carole would be healed.

Lucky, my little cat, leaped on to my lap, licked one of my fingers, and stretching out a soft furry paw touched my face. I hugged her close, and listened to my parents' muted talk.

'We couldn't bear our little one to die,' whispered my mother.

'No. I will go now to the church,' said the old priest, 'and pray.' And he whom I had thought was God, showed himself out.

What seemed a second or so later, my parents were looking again and again at each other, then at the child, in speechless astonishment and wonder. I, seeing the radiance of their faces and being newly initiated in the faith in so matter-of-fact a way, jumped from my seat, put down the cat and hung the toy mouse I was clutching on to the Christmas tree.

We were poor in those difficult years after the war, yet how happy! They seem, looking back, to have been one long summer of meals in the garden, blue skies and sunshine, bluebell woods, birdsong and the melodious meandering waters of our favourite brooks and streams, in whose reflection those untarnished skies of childhood lay.

Despite the pit wheels, slag heaps and shunting coal trucks, we were country children, and as carefree and irrepressible as children of the 1940s could be. What fun to watch the still occasional horse-drawn barge from the canal banks, to build houses in a hayfield, to run and walk and jump and skip wherever we wished, in freedom and safety. I can still feel the excitement too, at home, of coming across our mother cutting sandwiches in a corner of the kitchen on a Friday evening, and hear her, at our eager questioning, saying, 'Oh yes, we may be going to see Aunt Polly tomorrow.'

To this day I am not sure how real or mythical Aunt Polly was, yet she became a very good game. Especially when we caught Father the following morning at the crack of dawn, hiding buckets and spades under the picnic baskets in the back of the old side-car; and knew with a great whoop of joy that we were indeed bound for the seashore. As I grew older I pretended not to notice such things, knowing how much our parents loved to surprise us, though as young children we made them think of some very good reasons for taking swimsuits to Aunt Polly's.

Living on the borders of Nottinghamshire, and having the old motor cycle and side-car, meant that we frequently rattled off for the day into the Derbyshire Dales. I loved them. They were for me the heart of the countryside, and I early decided, leaning back against the warmth of a dry stone dyke and munching a piece of my mother's best slab cake, that the moment I was old enough, I would return to those beautiful hills to live; and if possible, until I had found the right farmer to marry, become a lady farm labourer.

Up until the age of ten, I had always thought that it was the worst of British luck to have been born a girl. Boys certainly, it seemed, had more fun, were braver, stronger and more daring, could become pilots, sea captains and mountaineers, and in all, life became for them just a huge adventure. Anyway, I was going to buy a motor bike, have a farm, and never again twizzle around on a table whilst Mother, with pins in her mouth, stuck them one by one into the hem of a dress I didn't want.

I feel full of shame now, when I think of the time she spent and the endless lengths she went to, to make the family income spin out. Whilst I, temperamental and ungrateful child that I was, went into an annual decline each time the much-practised-for Sunday school anniversary came around. Because I didn't want, I said, to wear a home-made frock of the same material and colour as Carole's, when my best friends would boastfully appear in bought ones. Yet I always did, and my sister and I, I am sure, must have looked very attractive.

As participants of a fallen human race there are many things that children as well as adults dislike, and one of my greatest antipathies, expressed in the form of a smarting, inner rebellion, was school on a Sunday. Nevertheless, the church itself held something of an attraction.

It was with the knowledge of its being a house of prayer deeply etched in my mind, that I attended the Sunday school at our village church of St James, though I remember little of actually praying at the Sunday school classes. Somehow, talking to God was a deep private affair, and something I only ever felt truly happy doing when I knew no one but God could hear.

One day, with great daring, and feeling uncomfortably naughty, I slipped in through a field gate of the churchyard, ran along its grassy path to the church and pushed open the heavy oak doors. Cautiously, peering this way and that, and before I could change my mind, I tip-toed down the cool sun-streaked aisle to the altar. It felt enormously large and empty, but I knelt down, whispered my prayer, and afterwards ran, with a joy I can still sometimes remember, triumphantly home to my mother and tea.

There was only one occasion when I arrived home to tea to find to my incredulity, the door locked and my mother out. Because of the unusualness of the occurrence I realised, despite my infancy, that there must be some unavoidable reason and so, unperturbed, sat on the garden swing in the sunshine to wait. Quietly I watched a little sparrow in the lilac tree, two others on the telegraph wires, and several in the hawthorn hedge. One hopped down to within a foot or so of the swing, and I told the others to come also so that I could tell them a story. To my wonder, though not, at that age, entirely to my surprise, they came, and more, and I told them how God had created the world.

What a rainbow of colour one's childhood holds, and how fleetingly it comes and goes. Many of these experiences my parents never knew, nor did I meditate much upon them. They were of the moment and just simply those glimpses that we in our tender years catch of heaven.

Standing up, I looked at the clock, gathered together what were the beginnings of this book, a confusion of papers, and drew the curtains against a darkening November night. The year was 1986, nearly forty years later, on the island of Fetlar.

It was 3 p.m. and the days were accelerating rapidly towards Christmas. Soon, here in Shetland, there would be little or no daylight and the biting winds would be laden with snow. It was warm and cosy by the fire in the thick-walled but room, where the sound of the rising storm was muffled. Flugga, with a plaintive miaow, brushed his silky body persuasively against the skirt of my habit, and I turned and followed his tail, triumphantly erect, into the chilly porch. There was still time to feed the cats, prepare a meal and re-draft the day's work before Vespers.

Clattering the saucers a little, as I lifted them from the floor of the room which serves also as my kitchen, caused an immediate eruption in the bedroom above. This was followed by a swift scuttle downstairs, Skerry, and a second plaintive miaow.

At 6 p.m., climbing the same staircase that Skerry had descended, I came to the second of the two small rooms in the

roof, the oratory. Bending in, I genuflected, switched on the heater, lit the candles and sat down. The skylight rattled and the little lamp by the statue of our Lady flickered in the draught that caught it. I was accustomed now to the howl of a gale lashing the thin felt roof, and the ocean's roar thundering over and over the rocks on the point. I mused upon life's rhythm and all its changing moods . . . upon this lovely isle, and how the beating back and forth of ceaseless tides, age after age, and the fierce storms, had formed the strange wild beauty of it . . . had eaten and beaten it to devious shapes, had seared through its most impenetrable stone to tear out those vast gurgling crevices and cavernous great holes. It was battleworn, and yet on a quiet day, at peace and imprinted with an indefeasible seal, a secret of its own, a sacred mark. A mark which was God's. Here in this tiny room — as the seasons circled around, the sun and moon, nights and days, months and years came and went — were the heart and core of it all.

The breviary lay open upon my knees. It was the season of Advent, full, like one's childhood, of that joyful expectancy and clear apprehension of a life evermore.

I knelt before the altar.

Come, O Lord, . . . that we may rejoice before Thee . . . with a perfect heart.[1]

2 Schooldays

School, I hated it, and Monday was always the worst day. I hated it all, first because I couldn't do sums, secondly, our very severe and unsmiling sewing teacher kept me on samplers and seemed always to be saying, 'Take it out and start again' – and thirdly, and hardest of all – I was painfully shy.

How I longed that our idyllic weekends on wheels should be interminably prolonged; and that, to me, seemed quite within the realms of possibility since our conveyance was somewhat unreliable. Yet I loved it, especially the side-car, which was to us young ones almost like the pumpkin in Cinderella, for miraculously, in the twinkling of an eye, it could be changed. Not into a fairytale coach but into the most tiny, most darling little bedroom on wheels. For Father had hinged the back of the front seat, so that with a quick click it could be dropped down and with cushions and a rug be made into a cosy bed just big enough for Carole and me.

You could, on those cool crack-of-dawn starts to the seaside, snuggle down and watch the clouds skimming above, the telegraph poles hopping along between their racing lines, or glimpse high red brick buildings and chimney pots, birds flying and tree tops waving in the wind. Everything zoomed past into the direction from which we had come, and it was only the flashing sunlight or the raindrops that accompanied us to our journey's end; that wonderful goal where my hunger for the sea would be satiated.

We never actually camped on any of our journeyings, nor, I suspect, were ever intended to, though at the end of a Sunday trip often I yearned that we should. How I longed, with my hands clenched tightly together, that we should be delayed overnight, even just once, in any of those strange exciting places, where so frequently it was our misfortune, or so my parents thought, to 'break down'. 'Please God, couldn't you possibly make it impossible for Father to fix it?' This was my constant plea, and it was not so much for the excitement of remaining in some beautiful scenic spot that I prayed thus. Just simply, that we might be prevented from returning home in time for me to have to go on the following morning to school.

God, though, took no notice. He neither responded nor sympathised with my predicament. Instead, He seemed rather to favour Father, who never failed to come out tops; for somehow, he always managed to get that crippled engine working again, and have us home in good time for bed.

Anything mechanical, my father loved, and during his army years in the Royal Electrical and Mechanical Engineers he trained and qualified as a fitter. After demobilisation he managed to get a job with a Nottinghamshire engineering firm, though finding just the right kind of work in that difficult post-war era was no easy task. Well aware of conditions, and by then having a family to support, he knew he could not quibble and so reluctantly accepted the job for seven pounds a week, as a fitter's mate. Unfortunately, the two men under whom he was mate were unqualified, and their work, or so my big ears had informed me, left much to be desired. There was no chance of promotion, and my father, a gentle unobtrusive man, was not happy. After a while, when no longer able to bear it, he began to look for other work – 'anything' – and finally found a job nearer home. In his new position his trade was not completely wasted, though sadly, to the end of his working days not a spark of satisfaction nor enjoyment did he ever find in it. His real happiness, as with all of us, was centred in the home. That home which increasingly inspired new and more colourful dimensions to my one firm intention to farm; which were, to grow up, get married, and be as happy as my parents were.

The arrival of an eight-inch black-and-white television just before the coronation of Queen Elizabeth II added for a while to our joy in life, causing great excitement. Yet it was a pleasure and expense we soon came to regret, for it ate into many a homely ploy, and cost many a cosy evening of being read to. Our parents, previously, had each evening read in turn a chapter of whatever book we might have had on hand – *Black Beauty*, *What Katy Did*, *Little Women*. Whilst we, usually in dressing gowns and sprawled by a crackling coal fire, sipped mugs of hot milk before bed. After the advent of that marvellous box of modern technology, we were instead converted to Muffin the Mule, Sooty and *Emergency Ward 10*.

One cannot deny, however, that the spectacle of actually seeing the coronation broadcast live was an unalloyed treat – and what an event it all was! I have never seen England so merry. Our whole village was festooned in colour, decked in furbelows, and for weeks before thrilled in a tremor of festal anticipation. Adults became as frivolous as their children could ever have been. They shouted from windows, waved from doorways, balanced precariously on top of porches, flung streamers across the frontage of their homes, stuck flags and tied balloons from gutterings and downspouts. The royal insignias, cut out of coloured paper, fluttered in the sunshine. Flower borders bloomed in red, white and blue and 'God Bless the Queen'. Young and old laughed and rejoiced. Tensing and Hillary conquered Everest, and best of all, we got a day off school.

Yes, those years were canopied in sunshine. Yet the day had to break when the clouds gathered and pain, that inevitable sharp blade in the process of growth, cut deep into my own heart. It happened one day after school.

The school bus ground to a halt. I jumped off and swung down the lane. There was so much I had to tell them at home. Carole would have arrived half an hour earlier, and would with any luck have had her say; and yes, it was the baker's day so perhaps there would be doughnuts. I broke into a run. As I passed under the first of two giant oaks something caught my eye. I stopped, glanced back, and what I saw sent my heart catapulting furiously into my mouth. There, shovelled off the road and out of the way though not out of sight, were the mangled remains of my little cat Lucky. Some hideous car, or lorry, or bus had hit her, and now she was dead, stiff and cold, could not be comforted, nor come at my call. I longed to feel the warmth of her in my arms, to hear her purr, to kiss her nose and to tell her how much I loved her. But what response would there be now? None. She had gone, far beyond my love or anyone's, and for ever. That was the pain of it. Her silky ears were broken. With leaden feet I turned for home.

The kettle was singing when I arrived and my mother greeted me cheerily. Everything was wretchedly normal, and I, newly ejected from the realm of normality, found all but my grief had been hitched out of focus. In the blur, though, I do recall that later Father went quietly off to collect the little body and bury it.

That night, after I had been perhaps more tenderly than usual tucked into bed, the tears began to flow, and racked with anguish I sobbed into my pillow. Something inside me hurt and hurt, gnawed and would not stop.

Several hours later with a swollen face, sore and my pride suddenly relinquished, I stumbled from bed. It was wrong to go downstairs at so late an hour I knew, though what now was a scolding when the rest of my life had been doomed to hell? My parents looked up, unsurprised and almost expectantly as I slipped through the door. Mother stretched out her arms and a second later, clasped tightly within them, I battled again to prevent

12

those infuriating tears from prising their way out. Father quickly made a mug of hot chocolate; and once a little of my equilibrium had been restored I was given my first lesson on death.

'Not even a little sparrow can fall to the ground without God knowing about it, you know,' said my mother. 'If we loved Lucky so much, how much more do you think God must love her?'

'He doesn't,' I said, 'because He wouldn't let her die or the sparrow or anything.'

'Oh yes He does. You've just learned that death can be a sharp and nasty and painful thing, but what you've still got to learn, and you may as well learn that today too, is that love, God's love, is a thousand, thousand times stronger.'

'And He,' said my father tapping out his pipe and crossing one knee over the other, 'has it all under control.' He explained that this was the whole point of Jesus' birth that first Christmas Day; and why later, when grown to be a man, He had died on the cross, and then rose again to show us heaven. 'It isn't easy to understand, I know,' he said. 'Even the very cleverest people can't see things as clearly as they'd like to, but one day we shall know, for sure and for certain, that all the time even for little Lucky it was all all right.'

My mother squeezed my arm. 'If only we'll trust God, and always, always go on loving however much it hurts, everything will be, and is even now, all right.' She paused. 'Did you say your prayers?'

'No.'

'Well, let's go back to bed and we'll say them together.'

So by that first necessary and painful pruning I began to grow just a little into the shape that the Master Gardener intended, and deeply comforted by my parents, was peacefully restored to bed.

My closest friend Valerie Farnsworth, a plump little farmer's daughter affectionately called 'Dump', told me excitedly one day that that there was going to be a course of confirmation classes in the old Reading Room.

'Will you come with me?' she asked. 'I'm going, because my mum wants me to be confirmed.'

'Yes, of course,' I said, 'though I'd better ask first.'

That night I did ask, and to my amazed indignation my parents said no.

'But why? Why not? Please let me.'

'Now just a minute, we think it's you who'd better tell us first why. Why do you think you should attend these classes?'

'Well,' I muttered, 'Valerie is.'

'That's a very poor reason,' said Father.

I racked my brains to think of another. 'I thought you'd be pleased.'

The silence was heavy, whilst demurely they waited, not for some profound theological protestation, but for a good honest reason for being confirmed.

'Well,' I said, still playing for time – and then with a sudden blinding flash of inspiration I had it. 'I want to belong fully to the Church.'

'And will you be faithful for the rest of your life and really honour the promises you make?' said Father.

Goodness, I hadn't realised what a serious business it was all going to be! 'Yes, yes,' I replied, determined now not to give in, and after an hour of tireless argument my mother laughed.

'If you really can promise that you will be a faithful member of the Church, and that means attending church every Sunday and abiding by all you are taught, you may, and God bless you.'

Some of the confirmation classes had been held in the vicarage and I had got to know and like our homely vicar's wife Mrs Newberry a great deal; and occasionally over the next year or so, I called in to see her.

Now that I understand better the workings of Divine Providence, I no longer find it strange that on a gentle spring evening two years later, Mrs Newberry placed before me a distinct choice of direction. There had been nothing more important in my mind than the imminence of the annual church sale. Then, suddenly out of the blue I was brought to a halt, and there, looming ahead was the first major turning point of my life. Gently, as if by an imperceptible hand, and through some strange pliant mechanism in myself, I was steered along a course which to any astute observer would have seemed totally out of keeping with my nature. Yet it was a course which I felt, though did not know how, to be irrevocably sure.

My whole being, even at that time, throbbed to create. Father had taught me the subservience of a pencil from the moment I had been able to hold one, and I drew, I painted, I forced my sister and her playmates to sit upon a row of chairs, poor wretches, whilst I brandished a bagatelle cue into their faces and made them sing songs I had written. I sawed and cut and knocked nails into wood. I designed a two-seater aeroplane too, to fly to the dales in. It stubbornly refused to leave the ground of course, yet my enthusiasm was never long quenched.

At fifteen I got a minor art scholarship to the School of Arts and Crafts in Mansfield fifteen miles from my home; and that was the point to which I had come as I stirred a wooden spoon around a mixing bowl, and listened to a sonorous clock ticking the minutes of an hour solemnly away in the Newberrys' farmhouse-like kitchen.

'Have you decided exactly what you want to do with your life?' asked Mrs Newberry.

'My parents want me to teach,' I told her, 'though I'm not sure I want to.'

'Yet you do like children?'

I pondered the question. 'Yes,' I said hesitantly.

She then put forward a proposal, painting my empty canvas with such artistry, and in such glowing colours that it could not fail to stimulate the imagination.

'These relatives of mine, they live at Felley Priory. You will have heard of them – the Oakes family . . . they have a castle in Scotland . . . private beach . . . boats . . . and a house too in Chelsea . . . theatre . . . river . . . walks . . . And they have a married daughter. She lives in Derbyshire, in the most beautiful house called The Cedars, in beautiful grounds. She has two dear little children and is expecting a third. She wants a nannie . . . Would you like me to arrange for you to see her?'

By the time I arrived home that evening I had already in my heart completely thrown overboard the rest of my schooling and accepted this glorious job. Though in all honesty and as I now see it, it was not so much the job, as its appendages that attracted. So with no little apprehension that night I approached my parents, and how unprepared I was for the bombshell that the excited proposal ignited. The anguished look upon their faces, which I can still see in my mind's eye, stunned me momentarily, and ever after confirmed the knowledge of how greatly I was loved.

'It is a bit of a sacrifice, ducky, to keep you on at school. The bus fares **are high** and the five pounds a term grant for your art materials is barely enough. Yet, as well you know, we don't begrudge you a penny of it, not one little bit,' said my mother. 'The greatest sacrifice we could make would be to allow you to leave home. We must all think very seriously about it.'

We did, and the next day they gave me their answer.

'If you really and honestly want this, then we can't in our hearts say no, and we'll go as far as looking into the possibilities of the work for you. If we like what we see, and you're offered the job and still want to take it, you may.'

So, very gently, the bonds of childhood and adolescence were broken, and my parents sadly yet firmly, and knowing they must, opened for me the gates to adult-hood.

I stirred the wooden spoon around the mixing bowl. The table at which I stood was in front of a small window that looked out across an ocean seething from the onslaught of a stormy night, tinged this morning with topaz as the sun, heavy-headed, and hardly able to heave himself aloft, began at last to make his low winter arc through the skies. Intent only, I thought as I laid down the spoon, upon dropping thankfully back as soon as he could into his liquid bed.

Never had I lost that first wonder of the sea, and my eyes now drank in a feast of colour and movement. The dark undulating waters heaved and rolled and gathered strength upon strength, to spew wave after wave of gilt-crested splendour upon the shore.

Opening a cupboard door, the one that creaked, I turned back to the window. Skerry, who had been furiously scratching a hole in the dark, damp soil pricked up his ears and resolved at once to

come in. His movement must subconsciously have reminded me of Lucky, for into my mind came the words of an old Advent antiphon:

Lift up thine eyes on high and behold who hath created these things.
Behold the Saviour cometh to loose thee from thy bonds.[1]

Through a little cat, long ago, I had first learned the reasons why Jesus had come; and now, with eager childlike delight, I looked forward, soon, to the commemoration of that coming in the celebration of another Christmas. Once again the infant Christ would offer our sin-sodden world the gift of salvation. 'Come unto me,' He seems to say year after year, 'repent and relinquish your hold upon sin, and I will open to you now, even in the land of your captivity, the floodgates of life, forgiveness, freedom and joy everlasting.'

3 Nanny

Any fear and apprehension on the day I went off to be interviewed for my first job must have been overlaid with excitement; the excitement of being driven in the Newberrys' roomy old Austin down a private road, that previously I had only ever sauntered past on a country walk.

Mrs Newberry was a comfortable, motherly companion and I felt happy and at ease as I sat back and enjoyed the spring leaves just unfurled, making intricate lacy patterns against a backcloth of blue sky. The pussy willow and catkins were out too; and as we rumbled down the uneven drive, around a sharp bend at the bottom, and by some attractive well-kept buildings that had once been stables, I caught the glimmer of a myriad of daffodils.

My attention however was quickly diverted to the magnificence of the rambling old priory. I was thunderstruck. Never until that moment had I met a house that could speak. Its tall shapely chimneys and windows of leaded glass, its quiet ecclesiastical air and cordial welcome seemed impregnated by the spirit of some long-forgotten past, and which in the strangest manner pervaded me. Its door was the key, and its walls jealously guarded, I felt, many a mystery and tableau of life and soaked up still the continuing cycle of its household's pursuit. We pulled up with a jolt, got out of the car and descended a flight of steps to the entrance.

The doorbell made a lovely reverberating jingle inside. Birds chirped in the nearby treetops, and a few daffodils rustled in an odd breeze that caught them. One gardener called to another across the grounds, and Mrs Newberry smiled an encouraging little smile across the step at me as

19

we heard a sudden light footfall somewhere within the precincts of the house. Soon there was a short rasping sound on the inside of the door, and it was slowly opened by a very young maid, who nervously asked us to come inside. I felt as though I were stepping into some sacrosanct holy of holies, and stood rooted reverently to the spot gazing around in awestruck wonder; and catching as I did so a whiff of Pear's soap.

'I'm sorry, Madam, but the Master and Mistress is both out at the minute. Would you like ta come in an' wait?'

'Isn't Miss Libby expected then today?' asked Mrs Newberry.

'No, Mam, Miss Elisabeth had ta put 'er visit off for today.'

'Oh that's a pity. Never mind. No dear, we won't wait thank you very much but we will have a little wander around the garden before we go . . . I'll be in touch, tell Mrs Oakes.'

Wandering around such a place was a new experience for me, and I tried to take it all in so that later I could tell Mum and Dad: the cook in her voluminous white apron peering just a little suspiciously from one of the kitchen windows . . . the stiff-looking and slightly bald butler flapping a green baize cloth through a door at the back . . . the trim, emerald-coloured, split level lawns with the pond below, beyond which nestled a beehive or two, and everywhere a profusion of daffodils . . .

'Isn't it lovely, dear?' said Mrs Newberry as we gathered, at her suggestion, an armful of flowers for my mother, and then returned home.

It was lovely, I agreed. In fact, I thought, highly elated, it was out of this world.

At tea-time a few days later Elisabeth James, 'Miss Libby', who had been visiting her parents at the priory, knocked at our door. She came in and chatted mostly with my parents. It was agreed that we should all pay a visit to her home at Tibshelf in Derbyshire to meet the two children, so one day the following week, after school, an expedition was made, and the outcome was that I accepted the job.

Several months later, washing a bucket of bleach-smelling nappies at the sink in the nursery bathroom I smilingly recalled a remark of my mother's.

'I don't know that this will stand you in particularly good stead for the kind of work you are going to do', she had said, fluttering an old school report in my direction.

I had found it whilst packing, and together we had perused its content: 'Patricia' – for that was my name before I entered the religious life – 'has made good progress in all but arithmetic.'

The list of subjects on the left-hand side and down which our eyes ran were headed by this abominable scourge; and there, in two neat little boxes running off to the right and in a bold scholastic hand, were the words 'disappointing' and 'erratic'. Quickly I dropped my eyes to the remarks at the bottom. 'Her art work is especially praiseworthy, her compositions are well written and very interesting. A little extra effort in arithmetic.'

I grinned. I had found this entertaining document amongst other old reports which had all said much the same thing. 'Needlework – quite good but rather slow. History – Geography – Nature Study – English – very good. PT and Games – fair.'

I tipped the soap suds out of the bowl. Now, I had had to learn a whole multitude of new domestic subjects, and my patient, long-suffering employer must often have wanted to cap the results, and perhaps did so in private, with the same remarks as my former teachers: 'erratic', 'disappointing', 'rather slow', 'fair'.

However, bit by bit, in most things I gradually improved, and found in fact that it was during those first early years at Tibshelf that my education, such as it has been, really began.

Elisabeth James always had her babies in the Westminster Hospital, and when Mark was born at the beginning of November we stayed, for the period of her confinement, at her parents' London house in Chelsea. Number twenty-five was a lovely characterful old residence in the corner of Oakley Gardens and had, as its address would suggest, a largish town garden.

I was enchanted with our stay for it was my first real encounter with city life, any city, and I remember it as being, to the raw country girl that I was, rather magical. Especially since in those long ago carefree days one could wander at will almost anywhere on a free day and really enjoy it. Sometimes I would go to a hairdresser's in King's Road for a three-and-sixpenny wash, cut and set. Or off on the underground to see the sights I had only ever heard of or seen on the television: The Zoo, the Tower of London, Marble Arch, and on later visits I would drift, just for the fun of it, in and around and out of Harrods; and once I had my portrait drawn by an artist in Selfridges as a gift for my parents.

On any fine working afternoon I walked with the children. Generally we trundled Tim's pushchair down through the garden, out of its stout wooden door on to the Embankment, over the Albert Bridge, through Battersea Park and into the Pleasure Gardens. Philip, who was four, and I, especially enjoyed this, though sometimes just by way of a change we would march off in the opposite direction to walk by the Serpentine.

Lots of nannies seemed to favour this area but they were mostly older and more formal-looking than I, pushing their elderly perambulators in a class-conscious, distinctly aloof sort of way; they rarely spoke. How nannyish they are, I arrogantly thought one day, pulling my coat across the tell-tale splashes of my own blue-and-white stripes. I rather hoped that they would take me for the children's mother, just doing a little stint whilst our nanny had her afternoon off. With a twitch at my scarf I pulled it ridiculously high; trying to keep hidden the

22

white starched collar beneath, and bending a little from time to time to discreetly tuck in the apron which infuriatingly sneaked out below my knees.

Yes, I would fit very nicely into that position. All I needed was a little more spit and polish and a rich young man. Perhaps I had been wrong about the farmer type. Still, I had only been a child when I had thought of that. I wonder which of these elegant houses I would choose as our town house, I mused; thinking, though, I would as lief live in Chelsea as here in South Kensington.

'Nanny!' A high-pitched, authoritative young voice jolted me out of my reverie; but it was only a petulant child about to pass by. He was wearing a pale blue double-breasted coat, pleated at the back and immaculate, and tugging endlessly at the sleeve of the formidable-looking woman who accompanied him.

'I want to see Peter Pan,' the voice complained.

'Yes darling, he's just a little further along the road. You love Peter Pan don't you?'

Mercifully, though my concept of mercy was pitiably weak, Philip and Tim called me Pat and not Nanny. Mercifully, too, we had just been along to see Peter Pan.

'What about going to the Science Museum?' I said to Philip, knowing that, young as he was, he adored it.

'Ooh rather, yes please,' he said, and we hurried off in that direction.

How I loved that autumn in London, scrunching through the leaves, watching the street artists, the pedlars, the old men reseating chairs and even the seldom-seen knife grinder. It was a new and exciting world.

In my later more sophisticated years the spotlights spun round and focused much more brightly upon the concert hall, the opera house, and needless to say the theatre. Only to add several more dazzling alternatives to an already mixed up bag of dreams.

Mark was born, and what a joy he was. Again Elisabeth James, his mother, was an excellent teacher, and

23

was always, I felt, exceedingly generous in sharing her children with me. By the time we returned to Tibshelf a fortnight later I was able confidently to handle and be responsible for in so many ways, that tiny child.

My employers, like myself, were Anglicans, and when at home in Derbyshire encouraged me to attend the local church. There, for a time, I joined the church choir. This gave me not only the stimulus of singing new music but also a second new and rather surprising enjoyment – that of wearing a kind of mortar board cap on my head and being hung about in a softly draped robe. Somehow I derived from this simple pleasure a feeling of 'rightness', though I could not for years conceive why. It was splendid though, especially as one walked up the aisle diverting the eye and singing lustily some processional or recessional hymn.

One day I was asked to sing the soprano solo in an aria from the Messiah. Inflated with pride I said I would and looked forward nervously to its performance. For a couple of weeks beforehand, on our crisp afternoon walks, with Mark in the pram, Timothy on the pram seat and Philip holding on to the handle, I went over and over the piece in my mind.

Down a rutted track to a farm we would trudge. The farmer had no objection to an occasional invasion of his farmyard, or to our leaning over the stall doors or cattle pens to discover tiny new calves or whatever other delight might await us. Often we stopped too, to talk to the beautiful long-eyelashed milking cows, to pick a wild flower or two, or just stare deeply content across the countryside. Hardwick Hall, which on a clear day could be seen plainly on its hillock in the distance, inspired me with many a new romantic notion.

'What is this life if, full of care,
We have no time to stand and stare?'

I would murmur W.H. Davies' well-known lines, recalled from school, appreciating greatly the truth of them. What a lovely, lovely world we lived in; and if so lovely, how much lovelier heaven must be.

I gave Philip a bunk up the bank to see the sheep on the other side, and was brought back to the import of the moment by a bleating ewe.

'And he shall feed His flock like a shepherd,' I hummed under my breath in the low tones of the contralto part; and then, 'Come unto me all ye that labour,' I jerked out, trying hard this time to get my own soprano bit right.

'Why don't you teach us a shepherd song too?' asked Philip.

'Yi not?' chuckled Tim.

'All right,' I replied and did. Suddenly noticing a row of blue noses, I looked at my watch. Yes, it was definitely, I decided, time for tea.

The great night of my debut came, and the triumphant success I had foreseen was aborted, I felt, by a puny and nervous performance. Everyone applauded me afterwards though, including my parents who had come for the occasion, and I dreamed that night of Covent Garden and of a glittering large-chested prima donna.

'While shepherds watched their flocks by night,
All seated on the ground . . .'

the children chanted excitedly a few days later around a huge Christmas tree in the large wood-panelled hall of The Cedars. It was Christmas Eve and before going to bed they would open their parcels by the log fire that later would be lit there. It was a pleasure that I sadly had to forgo, though only for the greater pleasure of going home to the bosom of my own family for the festival. One could not after all, all the time, have the best of both worlds.

It was Christmas Eve, and almost ten past two in the afternoon. Scraping a little ice off the inside of one of the back windows I peered out across the garden, up the long right-of-way that twists down to The Ness, and along the single track road that runs from one end of the island to the other.

There was still no sign of the young visitors I had been expecting. A little saddened I looked at my watch, then glanced hopefully back at the empty road. The sinking sun was casting a shaft of pink light over a distant hill. Soon it would be dark. Suddenly it caught in its glow something that moved. Could it be? Yes, two brightly coloured bonnets bobbing along. Hurriedly I fetched the binoculars, always to hand in a Shetland home, and breathing heavily upon the glinting pane rubbed a larger patch clear. Yes, it was Lynnie and Frances, almost now at the turning; and, good, coming into view was another gaggle of heads. That would be Brydon, Sally and Alison. There was the soft burr of a car coming nearer, not yet seen, and then another from the opposite direction. Soon, and only half an hour late — for we do not, I have since discovered, worry too much about time in Fetlar — the little croft house was full of children.

A short while later, switching off the lights, and getting the older children to keep an eye on the younger ones, we processed through the house. Clutching our candles we trod, through the passage and into the but, round the table and up the stairs, and at the top stooped in through the oratory door.

'Welcome, shepherds,' Joseph said,
'Push the door then bend your head.
Come in sirs, but gently tread.
    Yes you'll find Him here.'

'Angels told us, told us, told
That we'd find, a few hours old,
Christ the Lord as long foretold
    By the ancient seer.'

26

'Come in friends, you're all afright.
All you've seen and heard is right.
Here's the little Christ of Light
    Sent from heav'n above.'

'Ah, sweet maiden, who are we?
Rough and simple men, but see
Trembling now we bow the knee
    To the God of love.'

Breathless silence filled the air
In that humble stable bare,
Whilst each heart upraised in prayer
    Praised the Lord of Light.

Mary glanced then at each one
Tenderly as at her Son.
'Man's salvation has begun
    In this cave tonight.

'Many hearts with joy will sing,
Bells with merry peals will ring.
Ardent souls their love will bring
    Glorying in His birth.'

So the shepherds went their way,
Joyful that first Christmas Day.
Oh, what things they now would say.
    God had come to earth.

Our voices trailed away, and kneeling around the crib I knew
that Christmas had begun; for the children of Fetlar and for me.
    Later they ran off, flashing their torches, waving their bal-
loons and anticipating 'Santie'; and I, waving goodbye, came
in, washed up, fed the cats who had crept out from under a bed,

*and turned my thoughts to the evening ahead. Never before had
I brought in Christmas alone, and how strange it would be . . .*

*. . . Rising quietly from the prayer desk where I had been
kneeling I lit the lamp and then the altar candles. It was almost
midnight. Somewhere below the darkened skylight a ewe bleated
as I blew out the match and returned to the desk. The tiny
chapel, I thought, seemed full of people: islanders, friends,
relatives, loved ones and a whole multitude of others, earthly
and heavenly with me in spirit. I knelt.*

*'Oh God, who has made this most sacred night . . .' I began,
enjoying the flickering candlelight as it fell across the face of the
Christ Child,*

> *O God, who has made this most sacred night,*
> *grant we beseech Thee that we who have known*
> *the mysteries of His light on earth, may also*
> *have the fruition of His joys in heaven.*[1]

4 Scotland

We're going to Scotland
      We're going to Scotland
            We're going to Scotland
                  going to Scotland
                        going to Scotland
                              Scotland
                              Scotland

. . . the train wheels chanted, until we flew like the wind swift as an arrow, faster and faster, and my heart gave its hundredth lilt of excitement. Philip was fast asleep in the bunk above, and I below, snug and swayed into a happy daze, watched the brightly lit stations flip past. Timothy, and the baby Mark too, tucked cosily into his cot, were both in the two-berth sleeper with their mother next door, and we were all of us *en route* for Skipness.

In the middle of that afternoon, much to the amusement of the two older boys, we had prepared them for bed. Later, in gaily coloured pyjamas and dressing gowns, they had hugged their daddy goodbye.

'Yi aren't you coming to Skipness?' Timothy had asked.

'I am, on Saturday, Tim,' said his father, kissing him once more. 'You look after Mummy till then.' He had lifted them each on to the train, handed in the last bits of luggage and shut the door. 'Goodbye,' he shouted as the train slid out along the platform. 'See you at Skipness on Saturday. Good journeying! Love to Nanna. Goodbye, goodbye.'

Further and faster we had sped away, though only to draw nearer and nearer the attainment of that longed-for goal.

29

Whoever would have thought that Pat Millington would travel so far?

Bang, bang, bang, the Scottish drummer beat on his drum. Louder and louder he drummed, until it was so deafening I clapped my hands to my ears, and opening my eyes to entreat him to stop, saw at once where we were. The door clicked and, half-sitting and just slightly alarmed, I turned to watch it flung open.

'Good morning, Madam. Quite a pleasant one,' said a deep masculine voice, and to my wonderment a cup of tea and two plain biscuits were thrust inside. The door banged to, and all the excitement of the night before gushed back. Goodness, we must be nearly there, I breathed.

Scrambling quickly to the window to get my first glimpse of Scotland, I collapsed comfortably on to the end of the bunk, sipped my tea and savoured the magnificence of everything.

After that I could hardly bear for one single moment to unrivet my eyes from the scene as I dressed quickly. Those hills . . . my spirit rose to them, and wooded slopes, rivers and tiny waterfalls . . . they knit my heart in that hour and for always, to the splendour and lonely poignance of the land I had so longed to see. I was not to know then, of course, that it was nothing compared with the grandeur I would see further north. Or that later, whenever I was absent from it, I would feel an exile.

At Glasgow the train shuddered to its final halt, and the muted burble of the busy station seeped into our ears. Slightly dazed we tumbled out on to the platform and were welcomed warmly and at once by Elisabeth's father, Audouin Oakes, who had made the long and tiring journey from Skipness to meet us himself in the Rolls.

'Bobby!' shrieked the children, throwing themselves at their large, much-loved grandfather; and he, embracing them warmly, glanced over at us.

'Are you all terribly hungry?' he smiled.

A few hours later, and perhaps a little frayed at the edges, we arrived. What a wonderful, twisting and turning, in-and-out journey it had been – Loch Lomond, Inverary, Lochgilphead, Ardrishaig, Tarbert Loch Fyne; and finally our destination, which was a string of small cottages on the flounce of the sea. The narrow road wound its way between the cottages and the ocean, culminating in a cover of trees out of which rose magnificently the towers of Skipness.

We slid silently to a stop. Two or three of the staff quickly appeared to assist with the baggage, and passing in by the gun room we entered the main hall. It was a great deal larger than that of The Cedars, with the addition of a balcony and an elegant wide-sweeping stair. I was later to peer down through the bars of this same balcony and relish from my stance the savour of a real ball. As the prince of my dreams I chose a burly red-headed Scot. He was, needless to say, oblivious of the sixteen-year-old nanny tucked safely away in the shadows above. The main bedrooms ran off from the balcony. Beyond, were some darling little round ones in a round tower, and from these I always expected to hear humming forth the whirr of a wheel.

Upon our arrival we found James Oakes, Elisabeth James' elder brother already ensconced with his wife and young family. With them also, was their own very attractive nanny Josephine. Josephine was of an age with me and we had several times met, and liked each other, in Derbyshire. Now what a welcome she gave me, and what fun it would be sharing the children, the chores and our lovely nursery.

Duty time at Skipness was as pleasurable as time off, and since this was the case, we hardly bothered to draw a line. The mornings were mostly spent by the sea. We would borrow one of the garden Wrigleys, a three-wheeled truck with a small engine above its front wheel, and into this pile just about everything – picnic baskets, bathing suits, towels, buckets and spades, children and even ourselves, and trundle off to the beach, from where we could watch members of the household and their guests, going off to look at the lobster pots, or taking out the catamaran. Occasionally, and it was the highlight of our stay, Philip, Timothy and I would be taken out too, fishing for mackerel or off to the creels.

One beautiful warm afternoon I was at liberty to choose how I would spend it, and decided to walk. Clambering up the winding course of a narrow burn that plunged down to the sea, I breathed in a sudden refreshing and new kind of freedom. It was magical, I could sense that, though of a different nature from the magic of London. Here, under the roots of the stunted trees or behind this boulder or that, or up higher in the dark hollows of the hill amongst the tussocks of grass, could so easily live the little folk. A shiver of fascinated horror shot down my back. Perhaps the beach after all would be the more comfortable proposition. Half turning, I noticed to my left, a hundred yards higher, a ridge of stones and curiosity momentarily overcame any fear. Heading in a determined manner up from the stream, over the uneven ground towards the landmark, I saw as I approached, that it must be a sheep-fold. Yes, there was the door. The words of Jesus sprang to my mind: 'I am the door of the sheep.' Suddenly I felt safe.

Flopping relievedly on to the grass I leaned back against the rough warm stones, and gazed down over the glistening expanse of a quiescent sea. The sail of the catamaran had slumped in the calm, and the cottage roofs glinted in the summer sunshine. How lovely it was, and what good friends, I thought, I had already made among the cottagers – Janet McDougall, Betty McGregor and Betty's husband Jimmy, and wee Jamie their son. There, in fact was Betty, just a speck in the distance. She was hanging out some pieces of washing. Up here, just one step removed, I was at a great advantage, and at peace too. I closed my eyes, and my heart sang a wordless prayer that years later I was to discover, and love, expressed in written form.

Good Shepherd
be over me to shelter me
under me to uphold me
behind me to direct me
before me to lead me
ever with me to save me
above me to lift me
and bring me to the green pastures of eternal life.[1]

'There's going to be a real Scottish dance in the village hall tonight,' said Josephine greeting me excitedly when I returned, 'and we can both go if we wish to. Some of the family are, and most of the staff. Isn't that lovely? What are you going to wear?'

There was not a great deal to choose from and I cannot now remember exactly what it was. I do recall, though, that the evening was a tremendous whirl around, and that my employer's younger brother, 'Master Simon', jigged me through most of the dances and afterwards walked me home.

The castle grounds were beautiful and in them stood the ruin of a very much older building commonly known as the Old Castle. It was a square, solid, tower-like structure with a fortress-like feel. A narrow stairway ascended its floors to the top, and from there over the ramparts one could enjoy a magnificent view.

'All right, if you're so darn sure it's such rot come with me at midnight and prove it.'

Simon had been telling Josephine and me that the Old Castle was haunted, and we had laughed hilariously.

'Who is this woman anyway that walks "up and down, up and down" the stairway each night?' we had chuckled.

'Come and see,' he retorted, adding in the slyest of tones. 'Then you will know.'

That night, with one small torch between us, we met. The thought of the expedition had been a ridiculous joke. Now, as we approached the dark towering edifice, our knees quaked.

'Don't worry,' said Simon, forcing open the door at the bottom and stumbling noisily over one of the old baths stored immediately inside. 'You'll be all right with me, girls.'

Slowly we ascended the first flight of steps. I had overlooked the fact that it would be quite so dark. Also there was a fiendish nip in the air, and all manner of strange little noises.

'Shush,' Simon whispered, 'did you hear that?'

We stopped. We listened and cautiously, sliding into a more central position, wanting to be neither at the front nor at the back, I clutched at his sleeve.

We tip-toed silently on and up, hardly daring to breathe, with our ears strained intently for the slightest sound.

'Ooh-er! Help!' shouted Simon suddenly, throwing his arms in the air; and to our utter astonishment, and indignation, he turned, plunged rudely past the pair of us, and shrieked wildly down the stairs.

'Simon!' I shouted, 'The torch!' He had taken it with him. I was furious. How unchivalrous and cowardly, how . . .

'Oooh!' a soft, somnolent wail rose and fell in the shadows above. Losing not a second more I followed hot in his pursuit, despite the darkness, and with Jo on my heels.

'I heard a footfall and a rustle,' I gasped, as we toppled over the fence surrounding the Old Castle.

'Yes, so did I . . . Oh look,' she whispered and out of the dark ruin emerged not one but two ghostly sheet-like shapes.

They paused, hovered, and as we sped frantically away, flapped after us. We did not stop again until safely indoors where, having breathlessly tottered upstairs, we paused and leaned heavily upon a window-sill.

There, we peered blearily out into the inky night. The moon was no more than a sliver, though our eyes, accustomed by then to the gloom, saw a huddle of figures; dark, shadowy, bent figures. Bent? We stared harder. Yes, bent, bent double, and holding their sides.

'I say,' said Josephine, as the truth began slowly to dawn, 'd'you think we've been conned?'

Those glorious days at Skipness bowled by altogether too fast, and soon, back at Tibshelf, the autumn came and went so rapidly that before we knew where we were it was Christmas once more.

A few wintry days were spent at Felley Priory that year, which I thoroughly enjoyed for I could tramp home in the snow with or without the children. Mother had a very soft spot for young Tim, who was by then about three years old, and he for her.

'I yont to see your Mom,' he would demand with an engaging smile, and I liked nothing better than to take him.

Simon was at home on this particular visit and we turned the Felley drive into a superb toboggan run, racing down, each on a large toboggan with a row of screaming children upon our backs.

Half way up that same drive one day, on my way home, I turned to gaze at the Priory. 'Don't you wish you'd been born into such a family as this?' a voice in my head cajoled. Deep in thought I turned and went on, seeing myself for a fleeting moment being nervously presented at court, until suddenly my foot slid on a patch of ice and at once shattered the illusion. 'I must concentrate and watch where I tread,' I chided myself, regaining my balance.

The scene was like a Christmas card, and how silent it

was. The King of kings chose of His own accord to be born into a family like mine, I mused, turning the corner at the top of the drive; and pondering I scrunched on through the snow.

Christmas came and went. The months slipped past and soon, before we knew it, it was the holiday season again at Skipness. This time Simon took me netting, taught me to drive a tractor, played croquet with me on the lawn and billiards in the billiard room. Then, one moonlit evening, in a more romantic setting than even I could have imagined, with the sea at our feet and the hills at our back, he asked me to marry him.

'You must give me time, Simon, to think,' I said. In my dreams I had always said yes to the first eligible bachelor who had asked me, and now at almost eighteen I hesitated.

He pressed me for an answer, and how tempted I was, for what he offered I had come to enjoy, and indeed it was what I had thought I most wanted. I lapped up those rare occasions when with Master Simon I was addressed as 'Miss Pat'. I had adored having the wheel of his car; and how marvellous it would be to settle, as he had promised, in Scotland. I would never have to struggle as my parents had . . . and oh, so many things; though would I, could I be, ever as happy? Instantly I knew, and my answer to Simon was no.

Young Ewan was in the kirk with his mother on the Sunday before Christmas, and the next day, happening to meet his sister Alison who is a very forthright little girl of eight, I suggested that she bring him along on Christmas Eve.

'He would so enjoy the candles, and the Christmas crib, and the balloons,' I said.

She grimaced. 'He's bön nyargin' mam ta let him come for weeks.' Here she paused to crunch in half the sweet she was munching. 'Only he wouldna be göd if he did,' she said, and gave a delicious suck.

'He was an incredibly good boy in the kirk yesterday,' I said persuasively.

'That were only' – and here she glowered at me as though it were I indeed who was her little brother – 'because Mam said she'd skelp his bum if he wasna.' *

By a stroke of good luck I met Maggsie their mum in the shop on the following day, and after our brief exchange of conversation Ewan duly turned up on the twenty-fourth with Alison, clutching her hand, looking very pink and pleased with himself, and full of expectancy.

After our usual Christmas Eve ploys I now, instead of waving the children goodbye, go with them; and in the twinkling torchlight, or by the light of the moon, we sing carols around the crofts. This was instigated because no one within living memory seems to remember carol singers on Fetlar. Now we tramp from house to house, from croft to croft for as long as the children and I feel able. This year little Ewan was a stalwart and delightful addition. We sing a carol or two in each home, beginning and ending with a prayer said by the bairns:

> *Jesus in a stable: we love you, we praise you.*
> *Jesus in a stable: we worship and adore you.*
> *Jesus in a stable: we kneel down before you.*
> *This Christmas and for evermore. Amen.*

Mince pies and ginger beer are thrust upon us and later, delivered safely home, the Fetlar bairns sleep sound. I walk home, perhaps in the moonlight, tired also, but content and ready to prepare for the Midnight.

* On formal occasions the children can and do speak standard English instead of the dialect.

The gleam of distance, the gleam of sand,
  Roar of waves with a tide that sings
To tell us that Christ is born at hand,
  Saving Son of the King of kings.
  Moon on the mountains high ashine
    Reveals Him divine.
  Ho! ro! joy let there be![2]

5 Sorrow

I pulled up, very conveniently I thought, outside a hardware shop in the main street of a small market town between Tibshelf and my parents' home in Underwood. It was one of those bluest of blue autumnal days, though already there was a sharp nip in the air and a smoky scent of garden bonfires. I reached for my bag. It was the 7th October 1960, and also the twenty-first wedding anniversary of my parents. Their gift this time, I was determined, should both delight and surprise them. Mother had long had a hankering for some bathroom scales, and had I knew never been extravagant or affluent enough to buy them herself. These then were at the top of my list. A black cat curled in the open doorway of the shop stretched and yawned. Behind his sleek body I caught the glint of some hanging saucepans, a kettle and two garden spades. Yes, this was a shop where they might well be supplied. Clasping my bag to my bosom I bent from the car, slammed the door and walked a few paces to scan the shop window.

Hurrah, I chortled to myself, it must be my lucky day. For there, displayed for one and all to see, was exactly what I had had in mind – blue with a dash of pink and reasonably priced. Peering anxiously behind over a shoulder, to make sure that a row of equally determined purchasers were not about to pounce greedily forward and procure my quarry, I went in. The doorbell tinkled, and in two ticks I was out again with my neatly wrapped trophy tucked under my arm.

Half an hour later, sitting by a heaped up colliery fire at home, sipping a welcoming hot cup of tea, I laughed with my mother. I relished these brief exchanges when we caught up on every ounce of news we could think of – though they were of course only possible on the days I had the use of the Tibshelf car. We poured out and drank another cup of tea, and by the time that the Westminster chimes on the sideboard struck four, both Father and Carole were in.

Without further ado the aniversary gifts were torn open. What excitement, hilarity and exclamations of pleasure there were. I can still feel the hug of delight my mother gave me. It was the happiest of happy days, and as usual when the time came I was reluctant to leave.

'Only four more days though, ducky, and you'll be home again,' said my mother kissing me fondly good-bye, 'and so will we, in time for your birthday. Off you go, take good care . . . and God bless you.'

They were all, when I left, in rollicking spirits. Not through any celebratory inebriation, for we drank wine only at Christmas. Rather, for the exciting reason that enough money had at last been saved to purchase a car. Indeed on the very next day they were off to collect it. Luton, although some distance from our home, was the nearest town where the type of vehicle they wanted could be supplied. The one advantage, though, of travelling so far was that my father's sister and her husband and family lived there.

And this, said my mother, was a golden opportunity to spend a day or two with them.

On that grey, clouded Sunday whilst my family were away, I had to fulfil an engagement to preach. For, in the most strange and surprising manner I was, whilst still at Tibshelf, through the influence of a nonconformist friend, converted for the briefest period of my life into the Methodist Church. I was young and easy to impress and had in fact started a course that would enable me to become, as was my friend, a local lay preacher.

A lot of time had been spent in preparing a sermon for this particular Sunday and I was highly elated by its result. Certainly, it had not been the easiest of texts to choose: 'Weep not; she is not dead, but sleepeth.' Yet I had got it over, I felt, with great conviction.

After the service, having wished my goodnights, I made off to return to The Cedars. 'Bother,' I said pulling out the starter of the car several times over, though to no avail. The battery must have been completely flat. It was dark and freezing cold, and grumblingly I groped around for a good five minutes looking for a crank. When thankfully it came to light I marched with no little triumph, though with some slight vagueness as to exactly what to do, to the front of the car. Wiggling it neatly into a hole somewhere in the vicinity of the radiator, I yanked it around. Round and round I swung until reluctantly and very sluggishly, and just a little surprisingly, she started. Marvellous, I breathed, though my victory was somewhat swamped by a heavy and overriding anxiety that I had a long way to go.

'Eleven miles gone,' I murmured. 'Only two more now to go. Can I make it?' I was on a dark country road overhung with trees, and the car, most decidedly out of sorts, had taken every ounce of the will power I had, to be forced thus far. 'Please, oh please God help me to get there,' I pleaded, then chuckled, suddenly remembering how with the same earnest entreaty I had prayed as a child. Prayed then, of course, that my father would be unable to fix it. The boot now was on the other foot, and how uncomfortable it was. The engine coughed again, and the lights flickered. Desperately I pressed as hard and heavily as I could upon the accelerator, but no, she gave a final splutter and groaned to a stop.

The headlights had dropped unbelievably low, though nevertheless gave just enough light to crank her once more. Harassed, I flung round my arm, gripping the bar, and oh, surprise of surprises, she started! Hardly able to believe it I leaped in, released the brake and let the clutch slowly out. Though only alas, and how horribly sickening, to kangaroo in a most unbecoming fashion to the next junction. There, we shuddered to our final halt and absolutely no effort of mine would induce her to go. By then, however, there was a street light, and even more thankfully a public phone. I had had enough. In ten minutes Nick James, Elisabeth's husband, was with me, with the other car, a sturdy tow rope and a lot of charity.

The next morning a nasty damp mist eclipsed most of the daylight, enshrouding us in its heavy gloom. Mum, Dad and Carole would by now have started on their long journey home. Not much of a day for travelling I thought, though at any rate on this trip and in their new car they would be well protected from whatever the weather.

'Pat,' yelled Timmy from the cloakroom,' I yont my coat!'

'I'm coming,' I yelled back, thinking still of my parents.

Only the fortnight before I had been home, and not having had on that occasion the use of a car, they had returned me. The weather then, as now, had been shockingly wet; and the old motor cycle and side-car, no more reliable a machine than it had ever been, had made the journey back to Tibshelf a grim ordeal.

It had been late when we arrived. I remember it well – kissing their dripping faces goodnight, letting myself in and going immediately to bed. In bed I tossed and turned and wondered with each succeeding moment, where they would have got to by now. Then, oh so fearfully, and for no apparent or earthly reason I visualised an accident. An accident in which the most dreadful thing that could have happened, happened . . . so vivid was my fabrication of this incident that though I had never before been given to such irrational emotion, I wept, and cannot relate now the joy of my relief when I found in the clear light of the following day that it had all been some fleeting, ghastly and harrowing figment of the imagination.

42

Timothy tugged at my skirt. 'You didn't come, and I yont my coat,' he accused.

'But it's wet, Tim,' I said, and swept him off instead to play in the nursery.

It was at about 6.15 p.m. on the evening of that same day, the 10th October, that I shepherded the children, this time all three of them, upstairs to the bathroom. There I discovered rather irritatingly that I needed to slip down again to retrieve some item of clothing. As I descended the first few steps, the authoritative tones of the telephone reverberated in my ears. Libby, below in the kitchen, hurried at once to an adjoining passage to answer it. She smiled as I passed.

'Yes, Elisabeth James speaking,' she said, clapping the phone to her ear. 'Oh . . . how dreadful!   When?'

There was another pause. By this time I had reached the kitchen, found the missing garment and was moving back in the direction of the door.

'Yes, indeed I will,' she continued. 'Did you say Kettering?'

I stopped; felt the blood rush to my ears, and waited. 'You ought to be scurrying back to the children,' I told myself weakly.

Instead, feeling slightly cold, I moved a little nearer to the warmth of the cooker. The call was being brought to its final conclusion.

'Thank you so much for letting us know,' Libby said. 'Goodbye.'

The black polished receiver of the telephone clicked into place and, warming my hands on the hotplate cover of the Aga, I continued unashamedly to wait.

There was a hush, and an interminable few moments before Libby appeared. Her face was ashen, and it told me more precisely than any words what I had already guessed, though being a courageous person she came to the point at once.

43

'I'm afraid I've some rather bad news,' she began. 'Your mother . . .'

In her quick embrace she told me in exactly the words I knew that she would, that my mother was dead.

'She's not dead, no not dead,' a voice seemed to throb in my head, ' "but sleepeth".' I felt numb, and from what seemed to be the world's end I caught the resonance of Libby's voice.

'Your father and Carole are both in hospital badly bruised,' she was saying, 'though not seriously hurt. What would you like to do?'

'I'll go upstairs and bath the children,' I heard myself answer. How incredibly normal my voice sounded. I turned, and with heavy feet, and a heavier heart I went upstairs.

After a rumbustious bath time the children, clean and bobbish, scuttled, as was their wont, down to the library; and I, at that point being redundant whilst their parents took charge, returned to the kitchen.

'Oh!' I exclaimed upon entering the room. For there, sitting on its large central table, was Audouin Oakes.

It strikes me now that his daughter had probably alerted him to the turn of events and that he, being the kind of man he was, had instantly come. Though at that moment I assumed that his visit was no more than a casual call.

'Come here, child,' he said, and when I reached him he clamped a firm hand upon my shoulder. 'I want you to remember that "all things work together for good to them that love God",' he said quietly. 'All things do, you know, child, however dreadful they may seem at the time, if we really love God.'

I nodded. It seemed a cruel admonition under the circumstances and yet those words he quoted have stood me in good stead all my life since.

Mr Oakes offered to drive me to Kettering, where the accident had happened, and if I wished, to be at my disposal with the car for the next two days. 'And tonight,' he said, 'I think you should stay with your grandmother.'

I thanked him and he pushed me off to pack my bags.

The next morning at the crack of dawn, he collected me from my grandmother's house, and we set off, pausing only to pick up one or two items from the home of my parents. On the doormat was a mound of mail, mostly for me. Picking it up I flipped through the pack, looking only for an envelope I was sure would be there. My mother's; although she had been expecting to see me on this day – my birthday – I was certain she would also have slipped a card into the post, and yes, there it was. Slightly trembling I drew it out. We had both shared a passion for carnations, and her card was bedecked with them. 'A happy 19th, darling,' she had written. 'Van smashing. We are en route for home. From your ever loving Mum, Dad and Carole.'

They had stopped at a small store in Kettering, where, despite her troublesome leg, she got out, chose the card, wrote it, and posted it in a conveniently placed box. Three minutes later on the next crossroad, and with my father's name on her lips, she had died.

We arrived in Kettering just before lunch, and found to our great surprise that my father's younger brother, Uncle Alf, awaited us at the police station. He had generously made the journey from his home in Derby to identify my mother for me. We were three very sad pilgrims, yet found comfort in the strength of each other; and the police could not have been kinder.

After a quick cup of tea we went on to the hospital. Carole was still in a state of shock, bruised, and looked pathetic, limping off on the arm of my uncle and Mr Oakes. I watched them slowly make their way down a surgical-smelling corridor towards the main door, and then turned, and made my own way to a small side room where my father awaited me.

45

Pushing the door silently ajar I stared. Hunched on a chair by the side of the bed was no more than the faintest shadow of the man I had known. He looked up sensing my presence, and tremblingly stood.

'I'm sorry, so . . .' his voice trailed away. Instantly I, the stronger, embraced him, and in that moment grew up.

It was all a long-drawn-out and gruelling business. A post-mortem, an inquest and finally the funeral.

Mother had jokingly said on one of those happy occasions when we had sat by the fire and talked, that it had been a year of twenty-ones. This accident, our solicitor later informed us, was the twenty-first to have happened on that particular spot. Afterwards, and thankfully, it was made into a very much safer place.

I had never been to a crematorium before, and as we walked through its door behind the coffin, the deep voice of an organ playing the twenty-third psalm spilt into our ears. Mother had loved that psalm, and as the strains of it rose and fell I suddenly and light-heartedly felt glad for her, not realising then, of course, that it was probably played as an entrance to every funeral. We stepped slowly down the aisle. She's not dead, not dead but sleeping, I consoled myself, stealing a glance at the coffin carried high before us. Then looked quickly away. It was surely too small to be holding my mother. No, she can't be in it . . . Not dead, nor just sleeping . . . No, the air up to the very vaulting was vibrant with . . . What could it be? Her love? God's glory? God's glory was a glory, I firmly believed, as the organ strains swelled in a crescendo of triumph, that my mother now stooped to share. To touch with the tip of her finger my heart with . . . Yes, with its joy, torrents of it, until hardly bearable its wonder flowed over, and I, enlightened, saw at once from my own experience that death was only a door.

After the funeral we drove home to Underwood, for I had the use for a few days of a Felley car. I had already definitely decided to give up my job, and see my father

46

and Carole on to their feet. We stopped in a lay-by to have a drink, and relieved to have the funeral at last behind us, talked and talked.

'Do you remember,' I said reminiscing, 'how Mum used to call Carole and me for breakfast each morning with the words "Rise and shine"?'

'Rise and shine?' he said. 'Oh yes, I do.'

Eagerly I went on, 'And would you understand if I told you now that that is exactly how I feel. I feel bubbling over and ready to get on with it.'

He squeezed my hand, and starting the car, we moved slowly out on to the road.

It was surprisingly difficult, I found, adjusting back to the old life style, much as I had loved it. Often I felt cramped and stifled, and not a bit rise-and-shinish.

The Oakes family, not far away, kept a kindly eye on us all. The new local vicar too, more and more drew my father and me into parish activities. Carole, who had been so vibrant and fiery a teenager, remained pent up and strained looking. Mother and she had been alike in many ways, full of zeal, and her lack now of any real communication worried me. She was at that most difficult adolescent stage too, when a girl most needs her mother; and I, I knew, could in no way become a substitute Mum. If only she would break down and have a good heartbreaking cry, I complained. It took a worrying six months before she did. Though afterwards, she turned around, made a new and very nice friend, and got a place, as did her friend, in a pre-nursing school.

In our turn my father and I were persuaded first into the church choir, and secondly, and most stimulatingly, into the local drama group. By this stage I had to my surprise been thoroughly drawn back into the Anglican fold. The drama group was a real refreshment in spirit to us both and tremendous fun, and it had all started really with the vicar.

'I wish you would come along on Wednesday evening,' he had encouraged. 'We're still looking for a Miss

Gossage for *The Happiest Days of Your Life*.'

Borrowing a copy of the play, I had studied the part, liked it, wanted it badly and had gone along to the rehearsal convinced it was mine.

'Ah, come along in,' said the vicar opening the door. 'I'm so glad you could make it. I specially want you to meet a young friend of ours, Sheila Slack.' He introduced me to Sheila. 'She's going to be staying at the vicarage with us for a month or two,' he smiled; 'that is until she starts her moral welfare work training course in Liverpool. Only she'll tell you about all that herself.'

He left me with Sheila whom I liked at once, and despite the fact that she too was auditioning for the Miss Gossage part and got it, we soon became very good friends.

It was through Sheila's influence, for she had been brought up in the Anglo-Catholic tradition of the Anglican Church, that I made my first confession, and was introduced to such things as incense and church vestments. Previously I had regarded such adjuncts as 'Roman'. Now I discovered how greatly they added their own richness to the worship of God.

No, those months at home were not wasted in the bearing of fruit. Through my friendship with Sheila, through Audouin Oakes, who amongst his many accomplishments was an Anglican lay reader, and through Cyril Miles our kindly vicar, my knowledge of the Church of England was greatly enlarged.

'You know,' said the vicar one day, 'I believe that you would make a good Franciscan.'

'What's a Franciscan?' I asked.

'Here, sit down,' he said, pulling out a chair. 'Though tell me first if you know anything about St Francis.' He settled himself at this point comfortably in the chair opposite.

'Only that he preached to the birds,' I said, remembering a picture I had drawn in the infants class at school.

'Oh there's a lot more to him than that,' he smiled, and began to expound the virtues of this popular and much-loved saint. He told me how the Franciscan Order had grown and flourished, and how St Francis himself had introduced what is known as the Tertiary movement. 'You see,' he said, 'so many people wanted to give up their possessions abandoning absolutely all they had, to follow Francis in his interpretation of the Gospels, that he had to draw a distinctive line somewhere. For it was not, as he so clearly saw, a way of life to which God drew everyone. Some were, and were meant to be, married, though there was no reason why they shouldn't be attached to the Order in a looser knit way, and keep a simple rule of their own. Hence the Third Order of Tertiaries was established. I myself am attached to an Anglican friary in Somerset as a priest tertiary,' he said, and went on to tell me something about his own rule. He spoke of prayer, and of the refreshment of an annual retreat.

'What's a retreat?' I asked, and another hour sped by.

I left the vicarage, the same vicarage where the Newberrys had lived, with a sheaf of papers in a plastic bag, which later I flipped through, put aside and then into a drawer and forgot.

Feathery flakes had fallen from a laden sky tucking The Ness under a deep blanket of snow. Later the north wind had awoken, and with furious vengeance swept swirling gusts of the same white substance erratically into every nook and cranny, piling it high against the dykes, drifting it through fences, spilling it up the narrow roadways, plastering the croft house windows, billowing cloud after cloud of it over the banks and framing the cold, dark sea. Now, with the fury of the storm spent and the snow clouds swallowed up into the southern sky, the full moon was slung like a lantern over the isle.

My first intention was to start the engine of the old car, in order to re-charge the battery and prevent it from going flat during the extremely cold spell. Instead, smitten by a moment of lunar madness, I walked on over the frozen snows and down to the sea. There was no need of a torch, for the hills glittered like a milliard stars; and the isle, wrapped in silence, was swathed in a ghostly radiance, still, so still, that my footsteps spat and cracked like shots from a gun.

One star hung over the Hoga larger and brighter by far than all the others. Could it be less brilliant, I wondered, than that of the Magi?

Something flashed past. I stopped, listened, then looked quickly around and saw Flugga, rolling over and over in a snowdrift ahead. Glancing back towards The Ness I listened again. Could I have heard? No. I called and patiently waited. The grey outline of a croft house tucked neatly into the folds of a hill could be seen; its cosy golden-lit windows gave a heart warming glow. Ah, yes I was right. Once more I cocked my ear. There was the cry. It was faint and distant. I called louder. This time there was no hesitancy or shadow of doubt. A dark shape growing rapidly larger came hurtling towards us, tail in full sail. It was Skerry. 'Why didn't you tell me before, you were coming? Oh what an adventure!' he seemed to say and frisked playfully over and over, up and around with Flugga.

The star caught my eyes once again. Had their star led them on such a night as this to that holy Child who held within Himself all that man's heart could desire?

Behold there came wise men from the east to Bethlehem, and when they had opened their treasures they presented unto Him gifts: gold as to a great King, frankincense as to the true God, and myrrh for his burying.[1]

It was almost time for Compline, so crunching back over the machair I went in and up to the oratory. The bambino, his tiny hands uplifted, was still swaddled and lying in a bundle of hay in one corner of the room. I knelt. My star had led me also to the feet of the Christ Child, where day by day, month by month, year by year, I must needs lay the three same gifts.

Suddenly Mother seemed there and to smile down upon me. Words from the Epiphany Office came to my mind.

Arise, shine for thy light is come and the glory of the Lord is risen upon thee.[2]

6 Greenwoods

'Here's the form, Miss,' said a bespectacled young man, slightly older than myself, coming out from the office area of a car showroom.

I pulled off my gloves, took the form and moved towards a table where I had seen a pen. Looks reasonably straightforward anyway, I thought, bending over the document and filling it in above the dotted lines. Name . . . yes. Date of birth . . . yes. Good, I smiled, going on to read the smaller print that came next. 'Any person' it said, 'hiring a car from these premises is required to be twenty-one years or over.' Oh no! I gasped. I was only twenty. My mind spun round. What should I do? Pulling a glove nervously over the date of birth I had just written in, I glanced around. The young man was talking to a rather giggly female who had come in a few moments earlier. I was safe, at least for a while, to take stock of my dilemma.

My friend Sheila would be waiting for me, I knew, her bags packed and all other modes of transport that would have got her to Cambridge that afternoon, by now gone. It would be hateful to let her down, and such was my upbringing that it did not occur to me to change the date I had written. No, the only solution was, I decided, to carry on and hope for the best. Placing my second glove on top of the first, I completed the form.

'Is it the white car standing by the pump, outside the entrance?' I called over to the youth. Guiltily he jumped, and came hurrying towards me.

'Oh yes. Yes that's right. The Ford,' he said, still a little flustered, and bent beneath the counter to unhook for me a bunch of keys.

'I'm not too familiar with the idiosyncrasies of this particular model. I wonder if you would be kind enough . . .'

He nodded, jingled the keys in my direction and beckoned me to follow. Breathing deeply with relief I flipped up my gloves, snapped down the pen, and followed.

Once inside the car little time was wasted in getting used to its peculiarities. Thanking him, I smiled, and zoomed away with no more than a back thought in my head of the music which would have to be faced upon my return. How I could have done such a thing I do not know; though I think now that it may have had something to do with being young.

Sheila, armed with a picnic, was poised for flight when I picked her up. It would be fun, we had decided, if between us we hired a car and I drove her to the Mother and Baby Home in Cambridge. She was due to stay there for several weeks. Not to have a baby, but to do some practical work before beginning her course in Liverpool.

It was a lovely day, we had a pleasant run, and upon our arrival, the matron of the home welcomed us with a delicious tea. For me it was a most interesting, new and happy experience. I saw the home, the nursery, some of the mothers, most of the babies, and some of the staff. Afterwards Matron, having insisted in her matronly way that I rest awhile before setting off home, produced a lovely 'nosebag' as she called it for my sustenance *en route*.

The garage was expecting me to return the car punctually by half past ten, and making sure that I arrived a fraction earlier, I pulled up in a flare of lights in front of the sales room. I went in at once to hand back the keys.

'You're a young madam aren't you?' said an older man, who now loomed at the desk. He had a nice face, though an extremely angry one.

I wasn't used to being called a 'young madam' and my

hackles began to rise, though were promptly pressed back by a conscience that acknowledged he was right.

'You're under age,' he growled.

'You mean, hiring a car?' I must have sounded naive, though I found to my intense relief that it had the desired effect.

He scowled. 'See here,' he said, prodding a finger up and down, up and down, on the form I had filled in and pointing out to me the date of birth.

'How careless of me,' I said, bending over the document, lower than was really necessary to hide my blush. 'You must have been worried.'

The man grunted, and I went on to explain that I had of course hired a car before and that there had been no difficulties then.

'It's most embarrassing,' I said, standing up, and hoping by then that the fire glow had faded, 'especially when I thought that my main worry was keeping you up so late.'

Giving me a crooked smile he slapped my back in a conciliatory fashion, crumpled the form, and took the keys.

Not long after this incident, Audouin Oakes paid one of his intermittent calls at our home. Standing with his back to the fire, in a stance so very typical of him, he told us that that morning he had had a discussion on the telephone with an Anglican priest, the Reverend David Sheppard. David Sheppard was a friend of the Oakes family, and I had met him on one of my visits to Skipness when he and his wife had been guests.

'David was telling me,' said Mr Oakes jangling some loose coins around in the depths of a trouser pocket, 'a little bit more than I already knew about the West Ham Central Mission. Do either of you know of it?'

My father and I said we didn't, and he told us briefly how, founded by the Baptist Church for the down and outs of West Ham, its work had grown and flourished.

A large country house in Essex had been bought and opened as an experimental home, he told us, and had become a centre where all kinds of people in need, old people, unmarried mothers, people who had had nervous breakdowns and maladjusted children, could be cared for and helped. 'Though', he said, 'the thing that interests me most is the fact that it is run by a very young, inter-denominational staff.' Here he winked at my father. 'David tells me that they are looking for someone to assist the nursing sister who's in charge of the house, and to help with the children.' He paused a moment, gazing absently into space. 'We're wondering,' he said after a while, twitching an eyebrow in my direction, 'if you would be interested.'

I looked across at my father, for we had earlier been discussing my future along other lines.

'Carole and I can manage quite easily,' he said quietly, 'if you'd like to consider it. You've been at home over a year and I'm sure now that it's time you began to pick up the threads.'

It was true that my father was reasonably back on his feet, and Carole was happily occupied at that point with her ambitions to nurse.

'I don't know,' I ruminated, 'but yes, all right, I will consider it.'

Mr Oakes blew his nose, smiled broadly and patted my head.

A fortnight later I journeyed to Essex for the interview, and within a month had begun the work.

Snow still lay thickly in places and on my second day at Greenwoods, 'Padre', the Baptist minister who was warden of the home, suggested to my surprise that I go for a walk.

'It's far too lovely an afternoon to stay indoors if one doesn't have to,' he said, scrutinizing the scene through a nearby window. 'I propose that I take you and Abie into the surrounding area by car and drop you off. That way, you would see something of the local countryside, and also have an opportunity to make friends with Abie. He's a smart lad and it'll give him a kick to show you the way home. You need have no fears,' he added seeing the look on my face.

Later, as we watched Padre's car disappearing from sight, I fervently hoped I need not.

Abie was a sturdy olive-skinned Turkish Cypriot boy of about nine years old. His real un-abbreviated name was Abraham, and he was a handsome fellow, though determined, with a wonderful Cockney accent.

We trudged over fields, up public footpaths, and over stiles, chatting amicably enough. That was until, climbing a fence, we slid down a bank into a country road. It was narrow and, because of the tall oaks on either side, had caught little of the day's sunshine. It was deep with snow. Huge frozen lumps lined the indented wheel tracks, and were spattered by car-spewed mud. Abie's eyes sparkled, and bracing himself he pounced for the largest lump and proceeded to roll it weavingly in and out, over and through the deepest drifts he could find. In no time at all his snowball had assumed the most gigantic proportions and, barely able to push it further, he took the easiest way out, abandoning it in the road. I stopped. What a ghastly hazard it was going to be if left!

'Abie,' I called, 'let me give you a hand to move this super effort of yours to the side of the road.'

'No,' he said, thrusting his hands into the depths of his trouser pockets.

I was unused to children telling me no, though I felt that my new job behoved me to tread gently and patiently. Explaining the implications of leaving the frozen ball of snow in the middle of the road, I kept a frenzied eye and ear open for any signs or sounds of approaching traffic.

'No,' he said adamantly.

'I wonder how you would feel if I said no on an

56

occasion when you particularly wanted me to do something for you,' I said sternly.

'Cor,' his tone was incredulous, and skimming his nose with a sniff along the sleeve of his coat, he stared, 'Would ya really do som'in fa me?'

My heart melted. Poor little lad, he's not used to kindness. Here at Greenwoods, one obviously needed a gentler technique.

'Well, yes,' I said, 'I might.'

Then a sudden sneaky thought came into my head. 'Was there something particular you had in mind?' I inquired.

'Yeh,' he replied with another sniff and very tempted, I could see, to stick out his tongue, 'Fa you ta drop dead.'

And that was the end of that, or perhaps more correctly the beginning of my new employment. I made no comment, and rolled the snowball into the ditch myself.

Greenwoods was indeed a large country house, with an acre or two of surrounding field and woodland. It was a happy place, and the work not only great fun but broadening also in outlook! How well I remember driving a minibus full of shouting children and young people up to the Mission Centre in West Ham for some celebratory event. I wonder now, how at that age I had the nerve to do so; though perhaps the roads then were a great deal quieter than they are today.

On the staff was another Anglican besides myself, a nursing sister whom we called Sister Eunice, and it was she who introduced me to the parish church in Stock. It was a typical little Essex church with, if I remember rightly, a wooden spire. The simple proportions of the building were beautiful, yet what intrigued me most was the actual worship of its congregation.

I was especially enchanted by the little bell that was rung at Mass. Was it this Anglo-Catholicism that Sheila had converted me to, that so attracted? Just to walk into the church and sit down at the back in a pew, I found

uplifting, for the whole building had a deep and powerful feeling of prayer. I realise now that, due to the holy
old priest Father Tatham, the church was indeed prayed
in; and also the Blessed Sacrament was reserved there.

*I heard the sound of a car swerving round the tarmac in front of
the house. Father Lewis has made good time today, despite the
weather, I mused, stooping to light the oven. Blowing out the
match I closed the door and stood upright, silently congratulat-
ing my spiritual director on his accomplishment at having
arrived. The garden gate clicked, and quickly I pulled off my
apron and opened the croft house door. The wind howled in,
billowing up my veil and blowing out, I was certain, the
newly-lit oven.*

'Welcome, Father,' I said. 'Are you frozen?'

'No, not quite, though it is a bit rough,' he smiled.

*'I was doubtful whether the ferry would be running today,' I
said, forcing the swollen door shut and relighting the oven.*

*'Yes, I wondered that myself. How are you? Warm enough, I
hope?'*

*He went through to the but room and stood by the electric fire.
'I really think,' he murmured as I went in to join him two
minutes later, 'that we should begin to look for a second-hand
Rayburn for you, for in here. One hears occasionally of a cheap
one for sale.'*

*'It would certainly help to keep the house drier and warmer,' I
replied, touched by his kindness. Wondering, all the same, how
far a bag of coal would go — and how much it would cost.*

*We chatted awhile, and when Father was thoroughly warmed
through, we went up to the oratory.*

*'Grace and peace be with you from God our Father and the
Lord Jesus Christ. Amen.'*

Father Lewis stood at the tiny altar in the apex of the roof. A glint of sunlight sent a splintering shaft of light across the elderly white vestments he wore, then was instantly gone. It was still Epiphanytide, and the winter was yet upon us. Wind, snow — great lumps of it — and sometimes shine. The Mass continued.

'The Lord is King, the earth may be glad thereof . . .' said Father, now purely and simply priest at the altar.

'Yea, the multitude of the isles may be glad thereof,' my heart replied.[1]

The Lord is King. Yes, the King of kings here in our midst, and whom soon we would receive in the bread and the wine. A visitor to the oratory had said a few days before that he had found more atmosphere in the little chapel than in some of the greatest cathedrals. Our Lord, in the Blessed Sacrament, is here, I pondered. This place is prayed in, and the Mass is celebrated by a humble and holy priest.

Holy, Holy, Holy . . .

We began the Sanctus quietly together, and three times I tinkled the bell.

7 Joycroft

The house was small and full of books, and in its sitting room my eyes greedily devoured shelf after shelf: green books, blue books, red books . . . what should I read? This? or this? or even this? It was my day off, and I was spending it at Joycroft. Padre Bodey, and Gladys his wife, who were together the wardens of Greenwoods, devoted to our Lord, to each other and to the work they did, had kindly suggested I use their home if, and whenever I wished, for this purpose.

They had had the little house built for their own eventual retirement, and used it, two days a week, themselves.

'If you'd like to spend your days off also at Woodham you'd be very welcome,' Padre had told me. He had added too, most generously, that if I found my own way out there he would collect me at some point in the evening by car.

This I managed to do, by travelling on a rickety little train from Billericay, and here I was; and revelling for the very first time in my life in some leisure time alone. It was my first experience of a retreat, though I had not gone with the intention of using the quietude as such.

How I loved it! I would sit in the garden with a book, or by the fire indoors with a book. I would dream dreams with a book on my knee, or walk in the lovely country-side around, breathing in its quiet beauty, and puzzling, puzzling, seeking, seeking, my place in the world.

Ah, here was something interesting! The title of a book sprang out at me and filled my mind with the remembrance of those sessions I had had with Cyril Miles our vicar at home. It was called – and I poked in a finger and pulled it forward – *St Francis in the World Today*. Worth delving into, I decided, and placing it in a comfortable armchair I went off into the kitchen to put on the kettle for a mid-morning drink. Afterwards, cosily ensconced and sipping a mug of hot coffee, I began to read.

It was a short life of St Francis, and I have never since clapped eyes upon the same publication again. Nor do I think, perhaps, I would find it so stimulating if I did. Yet then, I was entranced. Yes, there was more to St Francis than I could ever have guessed. He had found – and could it possibly be what I myself was searching for? – perfect joy. Francis though, had found it through poverty, through giving everything to God. Every single possession he had. All his hopes, his desires, ambitions, his home and family, money and clothes . . . nothing had he withheld from God, and God had given back to him a hundredfold; and the world, it seemed, had followed him.

I laid the book upon my lap. That's all very well, I frowned, trying to sort it out in my mind, yet this is the *twentieth* century. I sank back into the comfort of the chair and closed my eyes. One would be accused of even greater madness than Francis himself if one went around . . . well, giving away one's clothes. Vowing oneself to holy poverty. Not, of course, that I had much to give away. Anyhow, I was a woman, he was a man, and a holy soul at that, called by God. I got up and went along to the kitchen to prepare a meal. A strange warm glow fluttered inside me. How silly I was. This afternoon I would go out for a walk and clear my head.

Carrying a tray back to the fireside I felt suddenly unaccountably happy, and savouring the sensation I quietly ate my lunch. This was one of the lovely things about being alone for a while, and was I supposed, what the vicar had somehow been getting at. A time set apart to relax, to think, to be with God, and to listen to what He might have to say. Surely, surely though, He could not mean me to go along the same path as St Francis? What of all those other wonderful, exciting things I was going to do?

Finishing my meal with a cup of coffee I re-opened the book. I reached the chapter about St Clare . . . So God had called a woman, after all, to this form of life. Slowly I turned the pages. Clare had been no more than a girl, a little younger in fact than myself, when she had seen and watched St Francis, and listened to him and his followers. She had felt as I was beginning to feel now; though she had had the courage to follow. I read on, becoming intoxicated almost, and fearful. If I were to contemplate such a path, I would have to give up my dreams of a husband, a home, a family, and Scotland. Yes, my beloved Scotland. Could the love of God compensate for such a sacrifice as that?

I closed the book, cleared away my tray, and pulling on a coat went off for my walk. The lanes and hedges and fields had taken on a sudden new hue. Even the people I passed were strangely different. I was falling in love; and little did I know it, deeply and for ever.

Padre collected me as usual that evening at about half past eight. As we rumbled back to Stock in his elderly car we spoke little, though often on previous occasions I had told him of my day's thoughts, or reading. Not tonight, though, I had decided, for I wanted to try it all out. To test it and see for myself if it really worked. And when I had, then perhaps would be the time to tell.

Once a week, on a certain morning and at a convenient moment, each of the staff would call into Padre's office to collect their wage. I kept a sharp eye on their comings and goings a week or so later, and chose my own moment well. Standing at a small table before him, I watched as he counted out two or three pound notes and handed them to me. I wondered how I should start. I cleared my throat. The speech I had prepared seemed inadequate.

'Padre,' I blurted out, 'I don't want it.'

Looking puzzled he asked in his gentle way the reason why. 'Sit down,' he urged, pushing a chair towards me.

Succeeding only in a stilted fashion, I tried to explain my intentions of testing the Franciscan way of life.

'Oh yes. Yes, I see,' he responded in a kindly tone. 'I'd like to know much more about it, though for the moment I'm afraid I must give you your wage.'

I stood up, staring at the money and did not speak.

'Look, I must give it to you. Let me do that, and then, when its yours, well, then you can do whatever you like with it, and if you want to plough it back into the mission you can.'

His eyes twinkled as I looked gratefully at him. I could have hugged him. Instead I picked up the money, said 'Thank you, Padre', and rushed away. I spent it on the children, the older residents, treats for meals, whatever I could think of; and being young and idealistic I spent it all. It was then, though, in a strange and mysterious way, that I experienced a joy I have never since lost. 'It works, it works!' I sang, and was over the moon.

Now, was the time to fish out and pore over those bits and pieces of information that Cyril Miles had given me regarding the Franciscan Order. Yes, I would ask to become a tertiary, I decided, and wrote at once to make the initial inquiries. Very soon a letter came back from the Mistress of Tertiaries, suggesting I meet her over a cup of coffee on Waterloo Station. This was arranged. Though I found, frustratingly and to my intense surprise, that when faced with the actual decision, I was unwilling to be tied. So the whole question of my becoming a tertiary was left in the air.

Before any of these developments, I had been nurturing a growing interest in the moral welfare side of our work at Greenwoods. Perhaps it was due to my association with Sheila, who had kept closely in touch. I loved working with the unmarried mothers, and had begun to wonder if that indeed was the field to which I should steer my course.

One day Audouin Oakes called in to see me at Greenwoods. I told him how much I enjoyed, and was becoming increasingly interested in, this side of the job. Keenly interested himself, he listened, and shortly afterwards paid a second visit. On this occasion we sat in the large conference room of the house and talked alone.

'I've paid you a second visit,' he said, 'because I want to talk very seriously with you about your future.'

We spoke of Simon mostly, and having ascertained that I had not changed my mind in that regard he offered, to my utter incredulity, to pay for my training as a moral welfare worker. My mind spun round. What a marvellous offer it was, and however could I have deserved it?

'It's exceedingly generous . . .' I stammered, 'and very exciting, yet I'd like to think more deeply about it first, if I may.'

'Do,' he said, 'though let me know reasonably soon.'

After he had gone I thought and thought. Is this really what I want to do? Should I allow him to do this for me? I could write to Sheila's matron at the Mother and Baby Home in Cambridge. I could ask if I might spend a holiday there working in a voluntary capacity. By doing that I would certainly have a better idea of what my answer to Mr Oakes should be. Oh dear, though, I remembered, I'm busy being a Franciscan at the moment, and have no money. How would I get there? What should I do? . . . And how does this Franciscanism come into it all?

The answer came a few days later when Mr Oakes, impatient to hear from me, rang from London.

'We're going to be in Chelsea for a few days,' he said, 'and wondered if you'd like to spend a couple of them with us. We could then discuss my proposal further.'

'How lovely,' I murmured. Then awkwardly explained that I couldn't really afford a visit to London.

'Don't worry about that, my dear, I could easily pick you up. The best time for me would be during the afternoon of Friday.'

We arranged a suitable time, and he duly arrived in the Rolls, and we slid up to Chelsea.

That evening, as I sat by the drawing room fire drinking a small liqueur, my kind benefactor pulled out a book from the pile of new paperbacks on the table beside him.

'Look,' he enjoined, showing me its title, *Religious Communities of the Anglican Communion*.

Tremendously surprised, I looked. Fancy Audouin Oakes, an Evangelical Church of England man, buying that. My heart drummed. Had he guessed of my own interest in the religious life?

Opening the book he ran a finger up and down its index, until he came to the entry he was looking for. Then, flicking the pages over, he found the passage and silently glanced through it once more. He handed the book to me.

'This is the community that interests me most,' he said. 'Read it.'

I looked at the heading, and the tiny glow inside blazed into a flame. Here were the details of a small Franciscan order of women.

'May I take it upstairs to peruse further?' I asked.

Later, kneeling at my bedside with the book spread open before me and at the same page, I read it once more. Slowly and thoroughly I read, and in that reading as in my heart, I knew that my destiny had been sealed.

Squeakily the service lift, in the form of a large trolley, rose through the dining room floor bringing with it a waft of bacon and toast. Plates were lifted off and placed on to the table and we sat to enjoy the refection.

'I've business in Cambridge today. Would you like to come?' asked Mr Oakes.

'How lovely,' I declared. 'I've an acquaintance in Cambridge I've been wanting to see.' It was somewhat impulsively that I made this statement, having my mind too much, I would think, upon the deliciousness of breakfast.

He looked up enquiringly and I told him about my idea of asking to have a working holiday at the Mother and Baby Home.

'A splendid idea,' he said. 'I'm delighted. So that settles it' . . . and taking the situation out of my hands, he arranged that I should go along with him. 'You can ring the Home when we arrive.'

How complicated life can get, I reflected.

We made Cambridge in very good time, and after some refreshment I rang the matron. The burr of the telephone droned endlessly on whilst nervously I waited for the receiver to be lifted. Just as I was about to place it thankfully down, a woman's voice caused me to raise it back to my ear.

'Hello . . .' she said, 'Hello. Hello . . .'

Quickly I explained who I was and why I was ringing, and again had to wait, this time for Matron to be fetched.

'Yes, yes,' she ejaculated. 'Do come along, certainly, though I can only spare you half an hour, and you may have to wait.'

I wished and wished that I had not rung. Nevertheless, ten minutes later Mr Oakes dropped me at the door of the Home.

I did have to wait, a very long time. And when she eventually arrived I thought that the matron this time, despite her smile, looked rather grim.

'Come into my room,' she said. 'I'm sure you'd like a cup of tea. I'm sorry you've been kept so long . . . it's been one of those days.'

I sat holding my cup and saucer and feeling very nervous.

'Sugar?' she asked.

'Yes please,' I replied timidly.

'Now in what way can I help you?'

She sounded very business-like.

I put my cup down carefully, and blushed, realising that she assumed my business was of another nature.

'I had to come and see you, though I don't honestly know why.' How feeble it sounded, and what a bad start when I was taking up so much of her valuable time. My colour deepened.

'Drink your tea and have one of these iced cakes. They're very good,' she said, beginning gradually to put me at ease.

I smiled. She smiled, and in no time at all I found, rather surprisingly, that I was telling this woman, whom I hardly knew, some of my deepest thoughts, and even of my notion of becoming a Franciscan tertiary.

'Yet,' I concluded, as unexpectedly to myself as to her, 'it's not enough.'

'You mean,' she twinkled now in full concord, 'that you think you've a religious vocation.'

'Yes, I think I have,' I said, admitting it for the very first time aloud.

'Well my dear, I'll tell you something now you've told me that – I too tried my vocation once at a little Franciscan convent in Devon.'

My jaw dropped. Could it possibly be . . .?

'That's the Reverend Mother's photograph on the mantelpiece,' she said, pointing to one of several framed pictures.

'Which Franciscan community is it?' I asked and she told me. 'It's the same one that I was reading about last night,' I divulged. Now there could be no uncertainty.

Matron smiled, 'Would you like me to write to the Reverend Mother for you?' she asked, and I said I would.

There had been a real whiff of spring in the air, and greatly content I tugged off my boots and came in. Having got several gardening jobs done, including the planting of the early broad beans, I was pleased. Now at the end of the afternoon I relished the thoughts of sitting down for an hour to do my spiritual reading. Washing my soil-stained hands, I changed into my habit, collected the books I would want, and sat peacefully down in the back of the oratory.

The dark simple cross with just a suggestion of the crucified figure carved out of a single piece of wood, hung against the white gable. I mused upon its form, hanging over the altar and between the combe sloped walls.

'If any man will come after me, let him deny himself, and take up his cross, and follow me.' These had been the words by which St Francis and his first two companions had been so enlightened. They had asked God to show them how He would have them live, what He would have them do; and to clarify what their hearts had told them, they had opened the Gospels three times.

At the first opening they had found: 'If thou wilt be perfect, go and sell that thou hast and give to the poor, and thou shalt have treasure in heaven; and come follow me.'

At the second: 'Take nothing for your journey, neither staff, nor scrip, nor bread, nor money, neither have two coats.'

At the third, it had been the passage about taking one's cross and following Christ.

This, Francis had told them, must be their rule, their way of life, and that of all who would follow them.

Those men, and St Clare also, I reflected, had given to God their all. They had withheld nothing, and 'all', as 'all' to me, had been given back to them a hundredfold. Even the very simplest material necessities given by God to us, are ours only to be held lightly and in trust.

I opened the Bible myself . . .

Furthermore then we beseech you, brethren, and exhort you by the Lord Jesus, that as ye have received of us how ye ought to walk and to please God, so ye would abound more and more.

8 *The Convent*

'Well, child?' said the Reverend Mother, bringing to its conclusion the talk we had just had. She bent forward, slightly rattling the rosary which hung from her cord, and did not wait for my answer. 'Would you like to look at a few other convents first?'

'No, Mother,' I replied at once. For what was the point when God so obviously had called me to this one. 'I'd like to come here . . . that's if you will have me?'

Mother, the Reverend Mother Foundress, elderly, imposing, with a silver wisp of hair struggling to sneak out between her wimple and her headband, turned towards a wide, flat-topped desk without rising. Picking up a sizeable diary, along with a pen, she flicked through its pages.

My fate now is irretrievably sealed, I told myself with a final burst of inward resignation. I'd done what God asked.

Looking around with renewed interest I noted a large crucifix hung high above the mantelpiece, a polished bracket supporting a statue of our Lady holding the Holy Child, and an open door. The door looked out over a picturesque garden where the day shimmered in the summer sunshine. Down a long expanse of lawn, which had an herbaceous border running up the length of one side, and a high rock wall extending up the other, I could see under the overhanging boughs of a great cedar, the smoky blue and green vista of a wooded glade. How peaceful it all was. The scent of roses drifted in, and a small tortoiseshell cat lay stretched out across the warm flagstones beyond the step.

'What about the fifth of August?' Mother asked, looking over towards me.

'Yes, that would be lovely,' I replied, not a little in awe of her. Ruminatively she continued to peer in my face, smiled, then wrote my name in her book.

The few possessions I had, which consisted mostly of books and clothing, I sorted out during the next few weeks, and passed them on to either Carole or Sheila. However, at the end of it all there remained one other item of which to dispose, and I did not know how. Something I had treasured, indeed clung to still . . . it was a box of Mother's letters. Was I to give to God . . . even those? 'Don't worry, you don't need to,' He seemed to say, 'though if you really love me as I think you do, you will.' I see-sawed back and forth. Those letters were all I had left of my mother. I read them and re-read and re-read again. They were precious. 'It's no good doing anything by halves, ducky, though,' she smiled from the lines, and a day or two later, clutching them closely to my bosom, I hustled out to the garden. At my father's bonfire site, making sure no one could see, I brushed the pack to my lips, and then with a determined enough hand though a trembling heart, I lit the match.

On the morning of the 5th August I left home. I had with me only the barest essentials I would need, and Father, accompanying me, carried my bag. He and Carole travelled as far as Nottingham to see me off on the Exeter coach, and for them and in the leaving of them, I had a dark foreboding. Yet it passed, and I was met at my journey's end and welcomed warmly.

That night I slept sound. I had been given for the week of my aspirancy a small room in the hospice part of the house. It had a large window which looked out over an attractive spinney of shrubs. The shrubbery sloped upwards towards the sisters' chapel, and whilst dressing that first morning I breathed in the exquisiteness of the rising sun catching the dew-dropped tips of flowers and leaves. The strains of the Prime hymn spilt through the windows of the old chapel, once a stable, and I listened enrapt to its undulating flow, intermingling with the twitter of birds. How upliftingly beautiful plainsong was:

Now that the daylight fills the sky,
We lift our hearts to God on high,
   That He, in all we do or say,
Would keep us free from harm today . . .[1]

What would this day and the rest of my days now hold, I wondered, as I waited for the house bell to ring. When eventually it pealed out its three chimes of three I tiptoed, hardly daring to breathe, along a passage, up and down stairs, over a boxed-in bridge, and through the cloister to Mass.

I loved my new life, and I remember for weeks going impatiently to bed each night with a longing for the next, and the next, new morning to break. To break and be gone and hasten on towards that wonderful day when I was to be clothed as a novice. I learned much of life too, and grew, and laughed merrily at the memory of my grandmother's face when she had gazed in stricken awe from it over the announcement I had specially visited her to make.

'Going to be a nun?' she ejaculated, standing in the sitting room of her home, in that little red-bricked row of houses where my story began. She stared unbelievingly, whilst I, with my eyes lowered, waited for her to recover her faculty of speech. 'Well, our Pat,' she breathed, 'I don't know where you get it from . . . It's not from our side of t'family.'

Before she died she managed to visit me in Devon and after that, for her, there was nowhere like it.

The date for my being made a novice was fixed. It was to be, I was told, the Thursday in Easter week, eight months after my admission as a postulant which had been on the feast of St Clare. The great day dawned and the sun streaked in through the chapel windows. I knelt before the altar, with the choir stalls, the Lady Chapel and the gallery behind me full of people, including my father. He had arrived the day before, looking, I had instantly seen, in need of someone to uncrumple him and care for him. A lump had caught in my throat when I had opened the door, though he had assured me of his well-being and happiness. Now he was swallowed up in the sea of faces behind. The habit I was to wear lay folded neatly upon the altar, and the priest officiating at the ceremony stood, his arms outstretched to bless it:

'O Lord God, Giver of all good gifts and generous Disposer of all blessings, we beseech Thee that Thou wouldest design to bless and sanctify this habit which Thy handmaid purposes to wear as a distinctive sign of religion, that amongst other women she may be recognised as dedicated to Thee. Amen.'

He lifted the bundle, and turning, stepped from the altar one pace towards me. Placing it in my arms he said quietly, 'The Lord clothe thee with the new man who was created by God in righteousness and holiness of truth.'

I accepted the burden, lifted it to my mouth, kissed it, and was then steered out of the chapel by the Reverend Mother. 'Jesus calls us, o'er the tumult . . .' the congregation sang tumultuously as the organ struck up, and I was led away to a private room. As quickly as possible I donned the habit, remembering with a sudden secret flash of amusement the choir robes at Tibshelf. The Reverend Mother pulled my wimple straight, smiled approvingly, and as the last verse of the hymn was being sung we re-entered the chapel. I felt whole and complete, though still a little nervous and shy, and absolutely in my right place. The organ and the voices ceased as I knelt once again at the desk, and the priest turned to face us.

'The Lord be with you,' he said, his hands outspread.

'And with thy spirit,' responded the people.

'Let us pray,' he continued.

'Look mercifully we beseech Thee, O Lord, upon Thy servant Sister Agnes and grant that through Thy grace, Blessed Mary ever Virgin, Blessed Francis and all Thy saints praying for her, she may persevere in Thy love and service until her life's end and finally inherit eternal blessedness.'

There was a tremor of relieved anticipation as my new name, Agnes, was announced in the prayer. I had known of it a few days before, though to most of the congregation my being named for St Clare's little sister, St Agnes of Assisi, was a happy surprise.

At the end of the service I was taken to greet each of the sisters, my father, the clergy and then all our friends. There were photographs, a festal breakfast, cards to be opened, and my Clothing Day, full of joy, was soon gone.

The following morning I hugged my father goodbye and promised to be home for my holiday at some point during the autumn. After that the days and months came and went and a new chapter of life began.

The convent was situated in the beautiful Devonshire countryside, on its own thirty-six acres of land, and very soon I learned the smell of the earth as I turned the rich red soil. I sowed seed, and planted, and harvested crops. I watched the seasons come and go with the steady rhythm of the Divine Office and the Church's year. I learned the crafts of husbandry and how to handle small machines. I swung a hook, thinned trees, watched the wisps of bonfire smoke swirl up between the treetops, mucked out and fed the pigs and poultry, and in my labours discerned the value of work.

I began also to grasp the art of living in community. A retreat conductor, himself a religious, had reminded us during the course of one of our Community retreats that those called to the religious life did not choose each other as companions. They were placed, he said, side by side in community by God. 'We are all like a collection of stones dropped into someone's pocket,' he had continued, 'rattling around until all our rough edges are knocked off, worn down and polished glossy and smooth.' Yes, along with life's necessary and unavoidable frictions, which helped fashion us to the form God meant us to be, there was great comradeship. Also, we had not only our work in common but our prayer, our adoration of God, our reading time and saying the Office. Silences too, the reception of the sacraments, and our recreational periods, were all meant to overflow, I felt, in a great outpouring of Christian charity to all who found their way to our home.

Often, the day spent, I would stand at the small window of the cell I used, and stare out over the dimpsy colours of a red, green and gold patchwork of rising hills. How those hills drew . . . had our Lady perhaps stood in as simple a chamber as this when God had sent His angel to tell her she was to bear His Son? She had been little more than a girl when she had accepted so simply God's will with all the sorrows and joys which were to come with it. Yet through her simple heartfelt 'yes', God had re-opened to His fallen world the gates of heaven. Should I go forward to vows? In my mind, and with joy, there was no other way.

My 'simple' or 'temporary vows' as they are sometimes called, when I was given the dedication of Our Lady of Joy, were made on St David's day 1966. They were renewed annually for three successive years until 1969. Then, on 1st July, the Feast of the Precious Blood, I made my solemn profession of life vows. I was by then twenty-seven years old.

The service of Solemn Vows on that warm summer day should have taken place at nine o'clock in the morning. Unfortunately the Bishop of Exeter, the Right Reverend Robert Mortimer, was caught up unavoidably in the House of Lords. It was the debate upon the Divorce Bill, and he was delayed until midday. However, the chapel was ready and waiting for him when he arrived, full of friends, relatives, candlelight and clergy, and of course myself. The service began and I was led again to the altar. In the making of these vows I was pledging myself, our Reverend Mother had told me, to the renunciation of all other and lesser loves than the love of Jesus. 'Excepting,' she had said, 'as we love other people in Him and for His sake.' I was affirming my desire, she had gone on to tell me, to become truly His servant and to be crucified with Him. I was attaching myself to the state of holy poverty, desiring in the name of Christ never to possess anything under heaven as my own.

The Bishop came forward, laid his hands upon my head, and I made my vows:

> 'In the Name of the Most Holy and undivided Trinity, and in honour of the glorious Ever-Virgin Mary Mother of God. I Sister Agnes of Our Lady of Joy make my vow to God to live in perpetual Chastity, Obedience and Poverty. I offer and consecrate to Him my person and my life, and I give myself up wholly to His Divine Love, to spend and be spent in His Holy Service.'

We were already halfway through Lent and the spring bulbs, even in Shetland, had spikes an inch or so high. Soon, I decided, I must get out the rotovator and tee it up in readiness to turn over the half-acre plot at the back of the house. Patches of snow still lay, and snowdrops pricked up their faces in warmer and more sheltered spots of croft house gardens. How quickly the rhythm of the seasons comes and goes, I mused, as I stared across the Wick and enjoyed the year's first warmth from the sun; and how ceaselessly the tides sweep to and fro reflecting the lovely spectrum of our constantly changing skies. Days had

rapidly begun to lengthen and soon our friends the oyster catchers, lapwings, larks, curlews and terns would be back. The rhythm of the Church's year too, and the pattern of prayer, reading and of the daily Divine Office, all formed the framework of the life in this place; playing their part in the great symphony of the glory of God, so richly outpoured around.

That night, extraordinarily late, my young friend Anne Hughson who lives and works with her parents on a neighbouring croft, rang up. Wondering who it could be, I lifted the receiver.

'Have you noticed the Merry Dancers through your back windows?' she asked.

'No,' I answered. 'The windows are frozen over. I'll slip outside.'

'Mam and Dad and I have all been out,' she told me. 'I won't keep you, though. You'll need to hurry.'

'Thank you, Anne,' I said, put down the phone, and flung on my cloak.

It was bitterly cold under the starlit sky, and the patches of snow upon which I stepped, crunched and cracked. Making my way to a suitable stance I leaned against a dry stone dyke and peered over. All thoughts then of any bodily discomfort fled. I gazed, enrapt, at the most awe-inspiring spectacle I have ever had the privilege to see. A quarter of an hour ticked rapidly away. I was oblivious of anything but the magnificence and splendour of the Merry Dancers — the Northern Lights —

leaping, cavorting across, and illuminating the northern sky. White tongues of flame-like light licked the hills as I watched, on that icy night, what seemed like a gigantic and silent fairytale firework display. It brought to my mind the words of Fra Giovanni, 'There is a radiance and glory in the darkness could we but see; and to see, we have only to look.' It was a humbling experience, almost too wondrous to bear alone.

I made my way indoors. 'There was darkness over all the land,' I thought, groping for the switch and thinking further towards Good Friday. Yet out of it came the most glorious light.

9 *Mothering Sunday*

Our Community was pledged to the observance and practice of the mixed life, 'giving the chief place always to prayer and contemplation', out of which was 'poured forth the fruits of contemplation in the active apostolate of the house'. One of the forms of active apostolate was conducting or helping with parochial missions in towns or villages, and on three occasions, during my twenty-one years in Devon, I assisted in the taking of such. On a fourth, I was asked to conduct a very simple children's mission myself, and during its duration to preach at the Sunday Sung Mass.

Although I had preached in Methodist churches in my youth, I was now full of fears. Addressing such a large, mixed audience would be a nerve-racking task. I had been taught, since my entry into the Community, to think differently and more precisely, and I now lacked the confidence and spontaneity of those early years. However, I was under obedience, and standing on the sanctuary step of the church of St. Thomas à Becket, Thorverton, I looked around at the sea of faces before me and felt my knees quake. In a frantic tussle with my memory to find the words with which I had meant to begin, I opened my mouth.

'It's often said that the hand that rocks the cradle rules the world . . .' I began.

How natural my voice sounded as I listened self-consciously to it, as though to some other person. Everyone in the congregation looked far too expectant; and could those back rows of, at the moment, attentive souls, hear? I raised my voice.

'I think that woman, womankind, doesn't always fully realise her own dignity and stature. For in her hand she holds great power, not only to rock the cradle but to sway the whole world for good or ill. "For," said St Augustine, "by woman came death, and by woman also came life." '

I looked over towards the back rows again. Yes, I was sure they could hear, for Dr Bedford was looking straight at me in an interested way; and those sitting in front of him, I could tell, were listening.

'By our first mother Eve's disobedience, destruction was born into the world. Yet, by the obedience of our second mother, salvation was given as a gift to mankind. For, when God sent the angel to ask Mary to become the mother of Himself she answered yes, when so easily she could have answered no. "Be it unto me according to Thy word," were the words which she spoke and they also are the words which God would have us speak, every moment of our lives . . .'

People are so afraid of saying yes to God, I cogitated, so afraid of the demands He will make upon them; and yet how easy it is, and what joy it brings.

. . . 'For we all have the same choice, to answer yes, or to answer no. To do, or not to do the will of God, and our decision influences the whole of mankind.'

I moved my weight slightly from one foot to the other, trying to remember what in my notes had come next. Oh yes:

'God made woman to be the helpmeet of man, and she can be the most wonderful and excellent helpmeet, or she can, and here again it is a matter of choice, be an unfortunate hindrance.

'We are told that women are the weaker sex, though a woman can if she wishes reverse the role and become the strong, dominant and proud partner of a marriage. Or she can, again if she wishes, be like Mary the Mother of God who sang in her Magnificat: "For He hath regarded the lowliness of His handmaiden." She in her humility was exalted, and so will every woman be lifted up, who is lowly. For in her weakness and in her humility is found her greatest strength.'

I drew in a breath, and at the same time a child began to fret.

'Indeed, perhaps there's supreme wisdom in the saying that the hand that rocks the cradle rules the world. For the hand that rocks the cradle implies, I'm sure, one who is lowly, and who better to possess our proud and disconsolate world?

'Today is Mothering Sunday,' I went on, and noticed as I did so various children beam up at their mums. 'The day we think of mothers with the deepest affection, and most of us have a mother to whom our thoughts fly. Mine is long since dead, one to whom I could go in time of trouble or jubilation, one who always understood, a place of refuge and a place of strength. A mother is usually the heartbeat of her family, the one who understands and cares and loves and suffers for her children. For through Eve's sin, suffering and pain became her hallmark; and she who is truly a mother accepts this stigma as willingly as Mary the Mother of God, her greatest exemplar accepted it, when she stood beneath the cross of her Son.'

The baby cried again and was unobtrusively taken out, and pausing slightly I looked at the sunlight catching the staunch pillars of the beautiful old church. I went on:

'So I think that a mother represents to most of us the place we call home, since in herself, in her physical make-up, she is a home, her womb being the first dwelling of her children. Mary bore God in her womb and that God now dwells in the midst of His body the Church. Mary's womb was a kind of temple that held within itself the glory of God, and our Church is a kind of mother which bears the same glory; and where we, who are that Church, gather today in the radiant stillness and peace of the presence of Our Lord. He who in a few moments we shall receive, and by whom we shall be nourished and fed, as He comes to us in our communion. To dwell with us for ever in the holy temple of our souls.

'Finally,' I said, feeling the surge of relief beginning to well up inside, 'let us look at the picture we've painted of a mother . . . of the soul who accepts with simplicity and meekness the Will of God for her, every moment of her life . . . of one who loves, and who suffers, if need be, for her children . . . of one who is always there, a place of refuge and a place of strength; and who bears within herself the glory of God. As we look at this picture,' I continued, 'we could be reminded of what we ourselves would wish to be, of our own mothers and what they are. Perhaps we will think of Mary the Mother of God, or of our own spiritual mother, the Church. Yet as we meditate upon these things I think we shall see that our meditation is incomplete; and how best can we complete it? By, I think, looking at the book of Revelation, for there we shall find the final portrait of a mother in all her perfection and splendour. It is of a woman clothed with the sun, with the moon under her feet and on her head a crown of twelve stars. Later we see her revealed as the "heavenly city, the new Jerusalem coming down from heaven and prepared as a bride adorned for her husband". This city prepared as a bride is the Tabernacle of God. It is the place to which we all travel, and where there will be no more tears, nor death, nor sorrow nor crying . . . A mother, under the shadows of whose wings we shall find our eternal joy. Amen.'

Buoyant inside, I turned, bowed towards the high altar, and walked back to my stall. The next hymn was being announced as I dropped to my knees, and I made my thanksgiving still meditating upon this state, this holy state of motherhood. My birthday, I had discovered soon after joining the community, fell upon the feast of the Motherhood of our Lady. That had been a piece of information which had pleased me enormously. I had once been so sure that I would marry and become a mother myself. Instead, and how mysterious God's ways and plans for us are, I had been consecrated and espoused to God, to live for the rest of my days a virginal life. Yet our Lady too was a virgin, I reflected, as I eased myself up to join in the hymn, and she had become the Mother of God. Could we religious then, given to God under our vows, share in some mysterious way this holy state? Yes, in homeliness, in purity, in simplicity, meekness, humility, pain and strength; and above all in love.

Easter morning was blue and the sun was so warm that I decided to take my breakfast out of doors into the garden. The islanders would think me very south of England, I chuckled as I sat on the raised plank which serves as a bench. Skerry companionably joined me, and scrupulously washed in a sliver of sunlight. He had had his breakfast, and after a night out, blinked sleepily up at four stiff-winged fulmars gliding round and around the chimney pot and over the yard — surveying my crust of bread, and the cat, I noted, with an air of palpable superiority.

A tiny wren fluttered from a boulder on to a strut of the garden gate, letting out a sudden clear, warbling trill, incredibly loud for so tiny a bird. Skerry, thoroughly alert now, and rigid except for a pair of quick darting eyes, ogled it. The wren, however, with a chirrup and a whirr of its wings, rose blithely in the air, and was gone.

Had the garden of the resurrection been so alive and beautiful on that first Easter morn? There had been a boulder there too, though many times larger; and a woman. Yes, a woman had been the first at the tomb, agonisingly trying to fathom the inexplicableness of loss. Yet the patience and strength of her love, and in her the love of all women, had been honoured by the first appearance of Christ; and was crowned in His making of her, Alleluia, His messenger of joy.

10 A Harbour

A waft of coffee and newly baked rolls drifted along the cloister and met me as I came out of the sacristy door after Mass. I walked over to the main building of the house. The gong was just about to be rung as I reached the hall, and there was an unusual buzz of suppressed chatter. I quickened my pace, as that ubiquitous air of joy and expectancy which could almost be touched, exploded into a peal of merry laughter and released an unrestrained waggle of tongues. The Reverend Mother had arrived, and teasingly had reproved a group of people waiting outside the refectory door. She had led the way in. It was Easter Day 1976, the house was vibrant with the air of festivity, and all customary rules, such as not talking in passages, breaking silences, and of silent meals, were to be shelved for the day.

The wooden tables, newly scrubbed, were decked with pots of polyanthus, daffodils and yellow primroses; and in each place, Sisters and guests intermingled, had been laid a down-turned card. Each card contained its own form of Easter greeting, and once the grace had been said, was plucked up with many an ejaculation of pleasure.

Guests to the house shared our meals and almost a dozen had come especially for the Holy Week ceremonies or to participate at the Easter Mass. The Reverend Mother, by then a later elected one, sat at the centre of the top table with, on her right, the Reverend Mother Foundress, fourteen years older than when we first met, and on her left, her deputy. Two narrow bench tables ran off down either side down the length of the room, and seated along these were the rest of the Community, visiting tertiaries and guests. Amongst this happy throng and with the loudest and most infectious laughs, sat Rosemary Thompson. She was a tertiary sister living at that time with us, sharing our community life when at home, though otherwise going off each day to do her job as a teacher at a school for the deaf. She had tried her vocation to the religious life before I myself had joined the Community, and as a novice had been given the name of Sister Columba. However, during the course of her novitiate she had discovered, and probably rightly, that her true vocation was in fact in the world working with handicapped children. Leaving the Order, she had kept loosely in touch, until several years later – and I remember it well – she had returned to become a tertiary member. Once back, and because of a continuing and deep devotion to St Columba, she had reverted to being called by her old novitiate name of Sister Columba.

Mother poured out a second round of tea or coffee and when the clatter of cups had subsided and more rolls had been brought from the kitchen, there was one of those surprisingly delightful lulls in the hubbub – 'of angels passing over', some would say – when folk peep shyly out of the corner of their eyes wondering who will be the first to break its magic. On this occasion it was the Reverend Mother Foundress who, slightly deaf, had not noticed. She was happily transmitting to her nearest neighbour, and without realising it, vividly to the whole room, her reminiscences and love of Iona. Someone clinked a cup. The spell was broken, and the meal and the general clamour of conversation continued. I gazed abstractedly across the room. Sister Columba looked up. Our eyes met, and in the most fleeting of glances I knew that together we would go to Iona; and more strangely, that in the going the course of our lives would be changed.

It was customary, at the end of breakfast, for each sister as she finished her meal to rise, bow to whoever happened at that point to be the most senior in the room, and take her implements out to the pantry. In the pantry she would wash them up.

Sister Columba was washing up hers alone when I arrived, and having a tea-cloth in her hands she kindly stayed on to wipe mine. As I thanked her, she nodded a smile, then involuntarily flashed out in an urgent tone, 'I'll ask Mother.'

That was all that was said. All perhaps that needed to be said; and later in the day, her telling me excitedly that Mother had said yes, came as no surprise.

'Since you have St Columba for your saint this year,' she enthused, 'and since most of the sisters have been to Iona, Mother thinks it would be a lovely idea – if I took you, I mean. I've offered to pay your fare, and it's to be in October. That's of course if you'd like to go. You would, wouldn't you?'

'Oh yes, more than anything Sister Columba,' I said. 'Thank you. Thank you so much.'

Yes, I had drawn my favourite Celtic saint from the Crib that year. Drawing a saint from the Christmas Crib on the Feast of Epiphany is a delightful old Franciscan custom, and one which reaches as far back as the saint himself. Forty or more slips of paper, each with the name of a saint written upon it, and a caption below of something the saint might have said, or is relevant to the saint, are folded neatly into three. Folded so, so that not an inkling of what is written can be seen, they are placed in the hay. Later, after the First Vespers of the Feast, the Sisters in turn and in order of seniority go to the Crib, kneel, kiss the feet of the Christ Child and take a caption from around Him. After this the tertiaries, or any other guests who may be present, draw their saints in their turn. It is the most thrilling occasion, and often the caption drawn is, one finds, of a very salutary nature.

October 7th of that same year at last arrived, and Sister Columba and I, bubbling with excitement were taken to Exeter to catch our train. It was a stormy day, and I was certain with each succeeding rainbow, and one after another did we see, that our holiday was to be a promise, and a part of something inexplicably meant.

We're going to Scotland
We're going to Scotland . . .

the train wheels began to chant; and swayed between the past and the future I sank back, closed my eyes, and thanked God.

We spent that night with friends in Paisley who drove us to Oban the next morning to catch our ferry. How beautiful the drive was, through hills and glens, around lochs, and over wooded slopes. I had returned to Scotland, and what a turn of the tide that was, after seventeen years. Never had I expected to be there again, and it felt like home.

In Oban, having bade affectionate and grateful farewells to our friends, we boarded the boat. Concentrating hard upon the precariousness of the gangplank, and making but slow progress, I heard the scurry of steps coming rapidly up behind. Assuming that they were about to pass by I squeezed to the side, and how great was my surprise when the two bags I was holding were unhooked from my hands and a courteous gentleman escorted me to the top. Thanking him copiously I wondered suddenly though how Sister Columba fared. Turning, I found her toiling up the last few steps. She was hung about with her usual accompaniment of encumbrances, red in the face and unassisted. The thought of her being almost twenty years older than I galvanized me at once into action, and I snatched her bags. She gave me a quizzical look, then laughed.

'It's surprising isn't it,' she puffed, 'what a habit will do for one? Especially if you're young.'

By late afternoon and after an idyllic sail we arrived at Craignure. On the pier waiting in welcome was a friend of the Community. She had a small cottage only a step or two's distance away, and there we were soon sat at a magnificent tea. It had been arranged that after some light refreshment she would drive us over the isle to catch the small ferry boat to Iona. We chatted, looked over her house and garden, and would have continued to chat, excepting she suddenly glanced at her watch.

'Goodness!' she exclaimed. 'We ought to have been on our way long ago.'

Without more ado we collected ourselves together, jumped into her car and zoomed over Mull. I was bewitched by the loveliness of it all and greedily drank in the beauty of the blue-tipped hills, bridal falls, the deer and the ribboned road that wound on and on. Our friend Mary tensely gripped the wheel until her knuckles showed white, concentrating, I could see, her whole being upon getting us there. She drove superbly.

'Only half a mile more,' she said, suddenly relaxing and swept gloriously around the next curve.

Alert, we looked, and I caught my first glimpse of Iona shimmering in a burst of sunshine. It was like some glistening jewel . . .

'Oh no!' cried Mary.

We looked at her alarmed, and followed her gaze.

'It looks as if the ferry's returning from its last trip over. Oh dear . . . Don't worry though,' she said, 'I'll have a word with the men on board.'

The one man we could see, stood darkly erect at the wheel, and looked, I thought as he manouvered the boat in, immoveably grim. Mary leapt from the car, and perilously, on the brink of the jetty, waved her silk scarf. He scowled, shook his head and slung over a spate of Scots words. Out of all this I deduced that he was finished for the day, definitely not taking us over, and that that was final. Despite Mary's sweetest pleadings, we were stranded. The man, adamant, turned his back, concentrated entirely upon mooring the vessel, and in due course, along with his pal, strode away.

Poor Mary, devastated and blaming herself, suggested weakly we leave our baggage where it was, and accompany her to the local shop. 'A friend of mine runs it,' she explained, 'and he may just be able to help.'

He was a kindly man, ready to give us any amount of his time. 'Tell you what,' he said, when Mary had poured out our tale of woe, 'why don't the three of you go into the café next door and have a nice cup of tea? Meanwhile I'll do what I can.'

Comforted by his cheeriness, we sipped our hot drinks.

'There's a huge crowd of people going into the Abbey,' I said after a while, peering in the direction of Iona.

'Oh yes, I know about that,' said Sister Columba.

We stared unbelievingly at her.

'Our landlady,' she quickly explained, 'with whom I've been corresponding, told me that she and almost everyone on Iona had been invited to a wedding. It's between a local boy and a local girl; and Miss Cameron said that since she would be attending it, and out when we arrived, we were to let ourselves in. We'll have to let her know, of course, of our delay.'

At that moment, our friend from the post office next door returned.

'Good news for you,' he boomed, beaming from ear to ear. 'I rang around and found, as I ought to have remembered, that there's a wedding . . . only unfortunately everyone seemed to be at it. Anyway, I was just about to give up, when the lady at the post office on Iona rang me back. She told me she'd just seen Bruce Wall walking past. He's a nice fellow, you know, who lives over there, and knowing he'd a boat and what a good sort he is she dashed out and caught him . . . Well, he said he'd be only too pleased to come over and get you, and he's on his way now.' He looked at our faces in breathless satisfaction. 'What about another cup of tea all round?' he urged.

Half an hour later we returned to the jetty, and in a sudden squally shower watched Mr Wall come in. The tiny boat bobbed up and down as we handed in our luggage, and looked exceedingly fragile on the choppy sea.

'Now,' shouted up Mr Wall throwing us each a yellow oilskin to put on, and sizing up Sister Columba with a twinkle in his eye. 'We'll have you first, darling,' he held up a hand, and steadying the swinging boat with his feet, gripped her arm.

Sister Columba lurched heavily down and was deftly and strategically placed in the now frantically oscillating boat. I, a skinny stone or two lighter, was adroitly seated along with the luggage on the other side. The outboard was started, and we waved at a transformed and radiant Mary, turned and roared into the Iona Sound.

Mr Wall and Sister Columba got along together at once, whilst I, dangling an arm over the side, only half listened to their piquant talk. It was about island life, birds, the history of Iona, and how to obtain permission to go into the Abbey library. My attention was far more excited by the bubbling cry of a curlew, the taste of the sea spray on my lips, and the colour of those hyacinth waters . . . Somehow I knew that the nearer we drew brought nearer the harbour to which since the day I had been born I had always been travelling . . .

'Call me Bruce.'

Mr Wall's voice jolted me back; and I gleaned that Bruce was, as he so descriptively put it, 'a refugee from Birmingham', that he had retired to Iona with his wife some time before, and that he was, during that present month, painting the outside of our landlady's house. He pointed over to a neat little house as he spoke, which we began to see more clearly as we neared the island. It stood some distance from the cluster of dwellings around the Abbey and was, as we knew, called Greenbank.

Greenbank stood on the edge of the sea, and that night

I was rocked to sleep by the sound of the tide washing the shore. That dear little shore of Traigmhor. Tomorrow we must explore its every nook and cranny . . . the sea . . . its roar . . . drawing back and fore the runnelling stones . . .

Hark the sea comes shoreward rolling,
Like a dear friend's step but softer,
With its wavelets rising falling,
Like the chubby cheeks of laughter.

Oft did I aforetime ponder
What might be their secret meaning,
Ferried from the ocean yonder
Towards the hard shore, shrilly keening.

As their music softly sounding
Reached my ear each moment sweeter,
Then I felt that awe abounding
Which no human tongue can utter.[1]

I stood on the Ness shore. Sea birds swooped and dived. A seal poked up its nose and then its head, twisting it curiously in my direction. The sea was like a mill-pond banded in every colour of liquid blue, pale blue and paler, paler to a silver sheen. A small boat droned out from the Wick into the open sea. It was too far distant to make out the figure who manned it. Could it be Harry? Or Andrew, Bob's son? Or Kenneth, or Mike or even Nick? It passed, until no more than the faintest murmur could be heard, or speck of it seen. Fetlar has no harbour of its own, so any fishing that is done, is done only during the summer months, and only from small boats with an outboard motor.

'Cast your nets on the right side of the ship,' Jesus had called out to His apostles from the shore on one of His resurrection appearances.

I sat on the shingle and leaned back against a warm boulder.

Sea pinks nodded from crevices of rock and carpeted the banks above, along with the wild violet and scabius. Soon the varieties of orchid would be out too, and all manner of other wild species of flowers. One was afraid, almost, to walk across the machair at this time of year, for fear of crushing such beauty. Few people of course ever found their way here. Visitors went to the obvious beauty spots, and the islanders were far too busy, or had other lovelier beaches nearer at hand to enjoy. Anyway, this one today was all mine . . .

Something pushed against me, and a furry ball curled into my side. I spoke to him and he flexed his paw and purred. A ewe nearby nuzzled two sleepy lambs and moved them on up the hill. 'Lovest thou Me?' The Lord had asked Simon Peter, and then had said, 'Feed my lambs . . .' and, 'Feed my sheep . . .' and, 'Feed my sheep . . .' That had been Peter's commission. I opened the breviary I had brought along with me. I would say the Second Vespers of Easter there on the shore . . .

Almighty God, who through Thine only-begotten Son Jesus Christ hast overcome death, and opened unto us the gate of everlasting life: we humbly beseech Thee, that as by Thy special grace preventing us Thou dost put into our minds good desires; so by Thy continual help we may bring the same to good effect.[2]

11 Iona

One afternoon after tea we resolved to walk west in the direction of the machair, our intent being to watch the sun set. The taste of salt was in the air and the muffled roar of the breakers pounding the rocks was psalmody to the ear, invigorating acutely one's awareness of that intangible holiness, sacred only to Iona. The sinking sun cast long shadows across the dunes, which flickered and danced, jumped, and joined a fleet of similar lights and shades which in turn blinked and fled away to cup themselves in the rosy curves and creases of the hills beyond.

We strolled above a ridge of opaline multi-coloured stones looking for a boulder upon which to sit, from where we could enjoy the last glow of the day reflecting its glory in the mirror of sea. A flock of sheep cropped grass close by, oblivious of us, the sunset, or the solitary one of its company standing stark and silhouetted on the Dun of the Fort. In the distance a swirl of screaming gulls wheeled and plummeted over an outcrop of dripping rock, looking for some tasty morsel of fish. We sat, and sitting, silently were caught up in that quiet sense of awe so wont to come upon one at the close of day. The last fiery nod of the sun sent a sudden violent shaft of colour across the water, setting the whole world ablaze. It subsided; melted into a thousand iridescent greys and pinks, and was gone. Yet still we sat, Sister Columba scrutinising the scene for the black head of a seal she had seen; and I gripped by the poignant stillness of the sheep on the crag.

That night I lay in bed intoxicated by I know not what, and listened to the gentle lappings of the sea washing Traigmhor. Back and fore, to and fro, its ebb and flow seemed to sing and to adulate God. A curtain fluttered. Love so gentle, love is like a tide that sings . . . I could feel the pulse of it beat with the rhythm of my own heart and then gradually, so gradually, grow louder. Louder, still louder, until the voice of it surged like a mighty flood.

> O Isle of Glory
> Isle of dreams
> The glory of God
> Upon thee seems
> To cleave thy rocks
> And hidden streams
> And kindle a holy fire.

The flare of that sunset we had seen illuminated the night, and in a cataract of glory thrummed through my veins; yet, only to subside, disperse and be gone, all that is, excepting the voice of it. Love, so gentle love, like a tide that sings; sings, rolls, swells, billows; deep and strong at the heart of it all. I listened, stretching my ears to hear. I heard. Then, awestruck, I slept.

Dawn broke and lying awake in a pool of sunshine I pondered upon the incredulity of what the voice had said. My mind reasoned, tussling it this way and that. I was crazy. The place had got a hold of me. Lots of people, especially religious, must have felt like this. It was, quite simply, a case of wishful thinking. Yes, that was what it was – wishful thinking. I was captivated by the place, enchanted by it, and now utterly carried away. How could God expect me . . . I hardly dared think . . . to bring the religious life back . . . here . . . to the Isles? No, I had got it all wrong.

Getting up I dressed and looked out through the window. A curlew was strutting around the garden gate. Its feathers ruffled in a flurry of wind and the smell of kippers drifted upstairs. I must hurry.

I knelt beside the bed. There was a long shelf above it,

and there, I had placed a triptych given me as a gift from Assisi. It usually went with me on holiday. I looked at it. Its central figure was that of our Lady holding the Holy Child. She would know the answer. I closed my eyes. 'Please God is it You or is it me? I must know,' I pleaded, 'If it's You . . .' I paused, then said the first thing that came into my head. 'If it's You, then let the island invite me. Invite me to return. To come back and live here, and let it do so before we leave.'

Good, I thought standing up a moment or two later, that should settle that little fancy. I felt better, and hungry, and hurried downstairs.

'Good morning,' said Miss Cameron. 'I hope you slept well?'

'Yes, very, thank you, Miss Cameron,' I replied, and pulled out a chair.

As we came to the end of the meal Sister Columba had a lovely idea. 'What about going to St Columba's Bay today?' she suggested. 'I think I could find the way, though it's some time since I last went.'

'Mmm, lovely. Just the day to go,' I murmured, biting into a piece of hot buttered toast. 'Look, there's Bruce Wall going past the window. Why don't you ask him to tell us the best route?'

Excusing herself, she gulped her last mouthfuls of coffee and went off. I cleared the table, and ten minutes later threw a borrowed anorak over my habit and slipped out too. She and Bruce were having some earnest conversation amid a conglomeration of paint pots at the back of the house; and when I called they looked up and laughed.

'Come over here, Sister Agnes,' Bruce beckoned.

Wondering what the urgency was, I skipped over. The wind billowed out the anorak, blowing the hood over my head. Sister Columba laughed. She was still laughing when I arrived, though Bruce had a look of gravity upon his face.

'Sister,' he began at once, 'I was thinking of you last night, and I was thinking, why don't you come and live here?'

I stared at him. This was too soon . . .

'Yes, I was thinking,' he continued, 'if down at the Abbey they can re-build . . . Well then, you . . .' and here he fixed me with his eye, '. . . could re-build the nunnery.'

I opened my mouth. 'But . . .' I stammered, and nothing more came. Eventually I managed to laugh as though it had been some little joke.

'Don't laugh,' he rebuked. 'I mean it.' And in my heart I knew that he did.

I did not tell anyone of this incident for years. Not even Sister Columba, nor did I relate to her that other thing which was so much a part of it.

Walking over to St Columba's Bay that same day I was smitten by the most peculiar feeling. It was as though my feet were being drawn into the very depths of the earth. A strange phenomenon, and one I had never experienced before, nor ever have since; yet convincing then, almost as though I were taking root. Continually I stooped to look. I wasn't, physically, of course, though that was how it felt, right up to my knees. The Isle had some inner fire . . . a fire that set my heart aglow . . . that drew my feet so deep that . . . I wanted to take root, to spring and to grow, to . . . to what? Whatever it was I could not penetrate the depths of it. Only God knew what it was, yet I would, if and when it came to fruition, dedicate it, I firmly vowed, to His Mother.

It was a haunting holiday and all too soon came to an end. One could hardly bear the thought of leaving; and on the morning of our departure I got up at the crack of dawn and went down to the shore. For half an hour I sat on a rock and watched the tide roll in.

Yes, it had been a good holiday, and during it Sister Columba and I had discovered all kinds of lovely things we had never previously realised that we had in common. She had spoken much of herself; of her disappointment over not having become a Sister, in the sense of having a religious vocation; and of a continuing desire to serve God in a deeper way. If she asked to try her vocation again, which I suspected she might, she would I was sure, be refused, on the grounds of age. The older we get, the more set in our ways we become; none of us is immune from that; unless of course she could become an exception to this particular rule. No, that would be too hard . . . Not impossible though, I chewed over . . . and I might just be able to direct her to an open door. No, I decided, I couldn't; it was none of my business. 'It is,' an inner voice urged. 'That is, if you've become as good friends as you think you have.' A wavelet broke on a nearby rock and splashed my toes. All right, I said resignedly, and spinning around slid down to the sand.

I knew that if the subject of vocation was to be reintroduced, it must be brought up whilst still on Iona; and since were were leaving soon after breakfast, it had to be now.

Sister Columba was late, and I inwardly quaked though did not, when she did appear, have the courage to raise the issue until the end of the meal. She looked at the time, rose and excused herself to do the last few things. Timidly, stretching a hand towards her I cleared my throat.

'Just a minute . . .'

She stopped.

'Are you seriously thinking of asking to try your vocation again when we get back?'

She looked slightly bemused. 'Yes,' she said, 'I think I am.'

'In that case there is something I'd like to say.'

She sat down eagerly, 'Go ahead.'

'We all of us,' I began, 'have a great many faults. Mostly tiresome small ones that don't seem to matter.

The trouble is, what people see of us outwardly, they judge of us inwardly, and that's a great matter if we're wanting to give our whole lives to God . . .' I took a deep breath.

'You mean I've got faults I've got to put right?' she said, an edge in her voice.

'We all have,' I replied.

'What are these outrageous faults then?' she boomed.

'You easily lose your temper . . .'

She glared at me, then saw the point and laughed. 'I expect I'm too old to learn new tricks. In fact I don't think I can.'

'No, not overnight, though what about a period of time, say three months? Then ask Mother. It's not that your own personal faults are "outrageous" . . . it's just . . .' I felt crimson with embarrassment, knowing how deplorable I was myself.

'I'll think about it,' she said in a tone of voice that made me think she might not, 'though now I must finish my packing.'

I went upstairs to finish mine too. There were a few oddments still to collect: toothbrush, slippers, Bible . . . Taking down the triptych from the shelf I looked at it; polished it with a clean hankie; considered, and returned it to the shelf. In thanks to God, I whispered. In thanks to Miss Cameron. And as a token of that something, I knew not what.

With hearts heavy for our own different reasons, we sailed from Iona. The overland bus was awaiting us at Fionnphort and we bounced over Mull back to Craignure. There, we boarded the Oban ferry. Never shall I forget the throb of its engines and how I felt, accurately as it turned out, that the next time I heard that burr and felt its vibration, and the lift of the waves, I would be on my way back to the isles. Often afterwards, in the fields, woodland or chapel, I heard and felt it, and knew that somehow it would come to pass.

In Oban we had an hour to spare before our train left for Glasgow. We decided to treat ourselves to a lovely last tea of doughnuts and gushy buns. Sister Columba looked over her teacup and smiled.

'It was very brave of you to tell me what you did, this morning. I'm grateful; and yes, all right I'll give it a trial.'

In those words a life-long friendship was cemented. We laughed, enjoyed our cream buns, and then went off to enjoy Oban in the time that was left.

One is far more aware of the wind, I have noticed, living in Shetland than anywhere else I have been. For it sweeps over us almost continuously, twisting and turning, tearing and tugging, tossing up anything and everything unfettered that is in its path. Over the island it swirls and into the sea. One learns to bend with it, contend with its strength, and in the end when it has dropped, miss it.

'Dere's nae draught ta day,' our friend Kenny will say

dolefully, and we know what he means. It dries the week's washing in ten minutes flat, though it needs to be firmly pegged! It dries out the ground. It lifts the waves and carries wood for our fires. It howls across the croft house chimney pots, licking the Rayburn fires into life; it puffs down the chimney pots and fills our homes with smoke. The Ness faces south, and I know now never to light the open fire in the ben room when the wind is north. Rosemary, once Sister Columba, who now lives in the other little croft house that stands on this point, has to watch for the wind blowing east.

'The wind bloweth where it listeth,' said Jesus, 'and thou hearest the sound thereof, but canst not tell whence it cometh, and whither it goeth: so is everyone that is born of the Spirit.'

12 The End of an Era

'D'you know what I'd like you to give me for Christmas this year?' I asked Sister Columba one day after we had been on a Community 'wash up' together.

'I can't think,' she replied. 'Something nice?'

Wiping my hands I unbuttoned the apron I was wearing and turned towards her. 'Yes, very,' I responded. 'I'd like you to write me something about Iona.'

Sister Columba, who had written and enjoyed writing since the age of about eight, ruminated upon the request. Although she led a busy life it would take her no time, I was certain, to produce something along the lines of a very short essay. Hooking my pinny over a peg, I left her considering, and walked through to the large empty convent kitchen. I was about to pour out two cups of tea when she also came in.

'You've really inspired me,' she said. 'Yes, I'll write you something, though only on one condition, that you'll illustrate whatever I write. That can be your gift to me.'

It was the end of November, just over a month since we had returned from Iona, and the time for racking one's brains had come. We had decided what we were going to give each other, within the Community, for Christmas. It had to be something home made, not rubbish, and attractive. Being vowed to holy poverty meant that one could not rush around the corner to a shop. Not that there was a shop within the radius of two or three miles, to rush around to. Sister Columba of course, being a tertiary and of independent means, could easily have purchased her gifts. However, she preferred, on the whole, to share in the fun.

During the days and the few weeks after, words

flowed from her pen, and the short piece of work I had expected, began to grow. Later, and to her delight, it was accepted for publication by the Iona Community under the title of *Columcille*.

'Would you like to hear Chapter One?' she asked me one day.

'Chapter One?' I queried in surprise. 'Yes, I'd love to; if I'm allowed.'

'It'll give you an idea how best to illustrate it,' she rejoined, reminding me in no uncertain terms of the stipulation that previously had been made. 'I'm holding you to it, and don't forget.'

I listened to her read in growing wonder, and suddenly knew what form my own gift should take. It would be a series of chapter headings of a Celtic design. What fun it all was, and how I looked forward to each recreational period long enough to get out my paints. It was a new experience for me to share an artistic project with someone else, and I opened my petals and soaked up the sun. Even so, I did not tell her of my call; nor of the reason behind my request.

Christmas came and went, and Sister Columba's little plan of working up towards asking to try her vocation again was put to the test. I was astounded at her vivacity . . .

Alas, though, God's ways are very mysterious, and when she asked to try once more, she was refused. Her balloon was pricked, and her desire to serve God frustrated. What was it then He was calling her to do? Patiently she went on; and how patient sometimes we have to be, waiting upon God to show us the way forward.

It was around this same period that I had word that my father was ill. Quickly a spring holiday was arranged, and I travelled up to the Midlands for a week to see him. An inoperable brain tumour had not at that point been diagnosed, though it was plain to see that his state was critical. He was up and down and in and out of hospital most of the time. My poor stepmother filled me in on the nightmare it had all been, and related to me also an interesting story.

'D'you remember your mum and dad having a little pear tree during your childhood years?' she asked one day.

'Indeed I do,' I replied, 'though it never bore fruit. Mum was awfully disappointed, and it wasn't for any lack of attention she gave it. She could be very determined, though, and when they moved house the pear tree came too. It was too big to bring really, and as far as I know remained barren.'

My stepmother glanced at the time, put down her shopping bag and sat on the edge of a chair. 'Well now, this is the strange thing,' she said. 'Last autumn, you may remember, Dad was taken to the hospital at Derby. He was having the most terrible nightmares and hallucinations . . . it's due to the pressure you know. One afternoon I went in to see him. He was all right that day, quite lucid in his mind really, though a bit excited. Actually, to tell you the truth, with his speech so slurred I couldn't tell, to start with, what he was saying. "Madge, go down the garden," was what it turned out to be. "There's three pears," he kept telling me. "I dreamed it, Madge, and I want you to pick them." "All right, Bernard," I said, just to pacify you know, and as I'm one that likes to keep a promise, it was the first thing I did.'

'And was there?' I asked.

'I'd never have believed it if I hadn't seen them myself. Exactly three . . . I'll have to go now love, the Co-op shuts at 5 p.m.'

Later, when we were alone, my father produced the last remaining pear of the three and presented me with it.

'I've saved this one for you,' he said.

Graciously I took the wizened, inedible-looking fruit.

'Strange, isn't it,' he continued, 'how these things

happen at the end of one era and at the beginning of another?'

On the last evening of my stay, Father and I were again alone. We chatted in the same way that Mother and I had so often done all those years earlier. The fire roared and crackled up the chimney; and I realised that apart from our farewells of the next morning it might well be our last colloquy on earth. It was, and in it, I told him about Iona. He was the very first person to hear.

'D'you think God really is calling me north?' I asked.

'I don't think,' he replied at once. 'I know . . . He is.'

In April of that same year, several weeks after my visit home, the whole Community caught a virulent 'flu germ. I cannot remember ever feeling so mouldy before, though I managed totteringly to stay on my feet. At the end of one morning I was busy, in the woolliest of fashions, doing a repair job in an outside workshop.

Clamping a piece of wood tightly into the vice, I thought of my father. He was so clever with wood, and had had great plans for the workshop he would have, and the carpentry he would do in his retirement. Now at sixty-two he was at death's door and was never likely to have that pleasure. I wondered how he was. A few days before he had been taken back into hospital, very ill. As I worked I prayed for him. How close he felt. His presence was almost tangible, and Mother's too, as though she were . . . waiting. I stopped, put down my tools and blew my nose. Metaphorically I held a hand of each of them. I wanted to lock them together . . . The hens at the top of the field cackled. I should really have been hurrying off to feed them. Peace, the sweetest peace, swept over me as the chapel bell reverberated over the countryside. I crossed myself and said the midday Angelus, though afterwards continued silently to stand. All was well, 'all manner of thing' was well with them. Deeply content I picked up the hammer, and then the last of my nails, and knocked it home.

An hour and a half later, after lunch, my stepmother rang.

'Dad's gone,' she told me, 'at about twelve o'clock.'

It was St George's day, and that evening I was asked to sit by the bedside of an elderly sister who also was dying. She had met my father on his rare visits to Devon, and had been informed of his death.

'Bernard,' she said as I walked into her room. 'How lovely for him. How I wish the dear Lord would call me too.' She beckoned to me to sit on her bed. 'I especially want to talk to you my dear,' she said, 'though could you ease me up just a little first?'

She spoke to me at length, of my own vocation, and of how she and the Mother Foundress, with whom she had started the community, had always believed in it.

'. . . and we believed it to be a vocation to prayer,' she said.

Two days later, on St Mark's day, she received her heart's desire, and died. Her funeral took place as soon as it could possibly be arranged, and the instant it was over I was taken to Exeter to catch my train home.

Father's funeral was the next day and the church of St Michael and All Angels, Underwood, was packed to the doors, mostly with miners. Shortly afterwards another service, one of memorial, was held. This was for the lay readers of the diocese, my father having been one of their number. The Bishop of Sherwood preached, and paid tribute to this gentle and unobtrusive man.

Thomas John had done many a kind deed for me when I was settling into The Ness, and it was with immense gratitude that I thought of him as I walked to the kirk. Three miles, up and down dale, it was, and that day I walked to his funeral. There were only two cars parked on the links, I noticed, as I descended the

last brae. I had arrived in good time. The little church sitting
below, was situated in one of the most lovely spots on Fetlar:
between Papil Loch and the huge crescent of Tresta's sandy
shore. Lambhoga rose up behind, and even on such a misty wet
day the scene had a magical look.

Having arrived early, I sat in the back of the kirk to wait. I
prayed for Thomas John. His coffin was already there, and a
sprinkling of people, though very soon and to my immense
surprise the church began to fill; not with a mixed congregation,
but with scores of men. I have never seen it so full. Where,
though, were all the women? Ah, there was Thomas John's wife
Hilda, and his daughter, and was that Anne? The service
started. I was later to discover that the male mourners had come
from all over Shetland, and that seemingly, it is still customary
for men only to attend funerals.

The Reverend Magnus Williamson announced the hymn. I
was used now to the form that a Presbyterian service took. Here
in the north, ecumenism is easier I have found, where first and
foremost the criterion, it seems, is to be Christian. The Roman
priest Father Gerald Fitzgibbon who was in Lerwick when I first

arrived, was a tremendous friend and stalwart supporter to me in the living of the religious life. We Christians here, believe that we have all of us much to learn from each other, and do.

It wasn't until the coffin had been carried out of the kirk by four bearers, including Thomas John's only son Anthony, and lowered into the ground, that I looked up and fully realised that I was the only female to have come out to the graveside. The men stood in the rain, solemn, ponderous, their caps doffed, while the final prayers were articulated. Magnus bowed his head and after a few moments' silence moved quietly away from the head of the grave. Caps were replaced, and I, beginning to feel slightly conspicuous, noticed that Magnus, his duties completed, was striding towards me, an arm outstretched. He was smiling and looking as though my presence was the most natural thing in the world; he was very kind.

Afterwards I walked home in the mizzle. 'Deep peace, a quiet rain to you;' I brooded, thinking of the words of the blind poet Alan Dall:

> Deep peace, an ebbing wave to you . . .
> Deep peace of the quiet earth to you;
> Deep peace of the sleeping stones to you . . .
> Deep peace of the Son of Peace . . .
> Deep peace of the heart of Mary to you . . .
> Deep peace . . .[1]

Deep peace, Thomas John to you. 'In the name of the Three who are One, Peace.'

Later I passed the croft house where my friends Mimie, Kenneth and Anne live. Mimie waved through the door.

'Come in and hae a cup wi' tae, Sister Agnes,' she called, and I went in.

13 Fetlar

'I asked you to come along and see me,' said the Reverend Mother, 'because I've recently received this letter asking if I would allow you to spend a fortnight's holiday in Shetland.'

Sitting under the veranda on a bench by her side I was transported with delight. Mother had received the letter from two retired friends of the Community who rented a small holiday cottage on the island of Fetlar. On several occasions they had regaled me with tantalising stories of their holidays there. Now, having realised how much I had enjoyed my Iona holiday, though not of course knowing the deep reason why, they had invited me to share a fortnight of their this year's visit.

'How marvellous,' I exclaimed.

'You can have overnight to think about it,' Mother told me.

'I don't need to,' I spluttered, thinking that if I wavered or took time the 'dream come true' might suddenly evaporate. 'I'd love to go.'

Plans wer^ made and on the 7th October, which would have been my parents' wedding anniversary, and which was the day that, seven years previously, Sister Columba and I had set forth for Iona, I boarded the *St Clair*. It was a fourteen-hour voyage up to Shetland from Aberdeen, and standing on deck I watched the evening lights of the city flicker on and then dance and twinkle in the busy waters of the dock. At exactly 6 p.m. the siren blew and the engines of the huge passenger and car ferry were propelled into action. I was *en route* for the isles, this time the Northern Isles, and my heart throbbed with the beat of the boat's powerful propulsion.

The next morning after breakfast we manoeuvred

alongside the pier at Lerwick. The blue sky and the houses of the quaint little town reflected themselves in the millpond of sea. The air was clean, clear and cool, and I gulped down deep snatches of it. Standing by my suitcase, I waited along with a host of other passengers for the gangplank to be pushed into position and the doors to be opened. What a surge there was when they were, and in no time I was at the ferry terminal buildings and boarding the overland bus. The bus, my instructions had told me, would take me north up the Mainland of Shetland.

It was a breathtaking trip, and one of the most lovely things about it was the friendliness of everyone. Every man, woman and child seemed so happy, and did not hesitate to pass the time of day. I had to stretch my ears though, often, to understand the dialects. The road wound on and on; around and up the side of picturesque voes, up and down treeless, sheep-laden hills, and past many an isolated croft.

The bus cassette enlivened this fascinating journey with jolly Shetland fiddle music; until to my surprise, we eventually came to a wide stretch of sea. There the road came to its end whilst, horrors, the bus unperturbed went on. On and up into a rolling ferry. The ramp was at once pulled in, and we were off once more, this time on a twenty-minute sailing to Yell. Once arrived, the ramp was lowered and we slid over it on to the isle. There, the bus terminated by the side of a slightly smaller bus, upon which most of us, with suitcases, haversacks, anoraks and binoculars, converged. Ensconsed in this charabanc we jogged over Yell, and an hour later, by which time I was almost the only passenger still on board, we arrived at Gutcher. Here a second little inter-island ferry awaited us and the bus, this time, reversed on to the boat to drop off mail for Unst and Fetlar. I, meanwhile, stiffly stepped out.

Settling myself comfortably in the bow of the boat I

looked forward, and my excitement by this stage knew no bounds, to my final crossing. It was fascinating; we sailed over to Unst then back to Yell; over to Unst again and only then on to Fetlar – and all for 10 pence! Having thoroughly got my sea legs by the time we arrived, I was able to walk steadily off the vessel on to the isle.

It was the 8th October 1983 and exactly seven years to the day since landing on the Isle of Iona; and perhaps I was, who knows, the first religious since the Reformation to land here.

The small croft house where our friends stayed had a splendid view of the sea, and as we sat with a cup of tea on a rough seat outside their window some short while later, I began to take in the only two other buildings to be seen. They were a couple of fields away and nearer the water.

'What dear little houses, and how nice you've got neighbours so close,' I said.

'Oh we haven't,' said my friends. 'Both houses are empty, and one in great need of repair. If you feel strong enough this afternoon we'll walk down that way and over on to the Ness beach.'

We enjoyed our walk, though how sad I felt! One of the houses, The Ness, had such potential, with outbuildings, half an acre of ground at the back and a tiny walled

garden in front. Alas, though, it had stood empty for two or three years, and already there was a hole in the roof. Part of the garden wall had fallen down, and that gate was hanging askew from a rusted hinge.

'This house,' said one of my friends, 'belongs to the Cheyne family; they own the large house we passed on the hill. You may remember we pointed it out to you as we drove from the ferry. The family, though, only come to stay on the island now for holidays.'

We walked on, and peeked at Lower Ness too. It stood a few hundred feet away, sideways on, and on slightly lower ground. This house, I felt, had gone far beyond repair; and why was I worrying? It was nothing to do with me. I was a sister bound to God by my vows, and to my Community. Never would I be in a position to save the life of two little houses, or even one. Only Community business was my business, and the Community, I knew, would never contemplate such a thing. We went on the short distance down to the beach, then doing a circular tour via a ring of stones, the remains of a round house and a stone row, we returned to their cottage.

The next morning, calling in at the island shop, I bought two or three postcards. Later in the day I wrote them. This holiday, I decided, I would send greetings to our chaplain. Carefully I chose the card I thought he would most like, and in the evening posted it. I little realised how such a small act was going to play so vital a role in the changing of my life.

I stood quietly on the old chapel site of Halliara-kirk. It was my last day on Fetlar and I had wanted a second time to return to this spot. It had a very special feel, I sensed, conducive to prayer, and had retained from who knows how many years ago the atmosphere of something sacred. A cold wind clutched at my cloak, and wrapping it more closely around me I perched on one of the scattered stones. Had a hermit perhaps lived here long ago? Why had it been dedicated to St Hilary, or perhaps it was St Hilarion? Had it been the church for this area of the island? Certainly it commanded a magnificent view. South over The Ness, east to Funzie and Everland, west over Houbie and to Tresta, and north to the Vord Hill; one could see the sea on almost every side. Why, though . . .? Why . . .? Why . . .? So many questions, and why was I so magnetised to the Isles . . .? Only the last question was I able to answer, and that now, without a shadow of a doubt. I was magnetised because God was calling me to them.

That same call had come again, and exactly as I had received it on Iona, though this time a decision had had to be made. God had seemed to say, 'You may answer yes, or you may answer no. It's your own choice, though if you answer no, it will be the end of your vocation as it is meant to be, and I shall ask you no more.' I had spent a whole night agonising over it, trying to summon up the courage to do what God asked. By the morning I had made up my mind, and knew now that for sure and certain and whatever the cost, there could be no going back. My answer was yes.

I rose from my boulder, walked a few steps and there I stood facing what could have been the altar end of a small chapel, now a ruin. Had it been a chapel? Or just some small building to shelter the sheep? Whatever the answer the Great Shepherd was there. I knelt . . .

Good Shepherd
be over me to shelter me
under me to uphold me
behind me to direct me . . .[1]

Now I must go back to Devon and ask permission. I crossed myself. 'In the Name of the Three who are One, the Father, the Son and the Holy Ghost. Amen.'

The sun was high in the sky and really warm on the hill up here at Halliara-kirk. The world shimmered below. I had lived on Fetlar now for over two years. How neat and cared for The Ness looked, with its rows of vegetables filling most of the half-acre yard at the back, its lawns cut, roofs repaired, and the sea like our Lady's mantle swathed out behind. The byre was going to convert into the most lovely chapel when I had a little more time and soon, I hoped, Bob would be erecting the bell. The bell had been given me by the people of Fetlar from the old East Kirk. I had been touched by the gift, and long for the day when its tongue will ring out again daily over the isle.

As my eye swept the scene, a flicker of movement caught my gaze. It was on the long right-of-way which winds down to The Ness. I shaded my eyes. Ah, Rosemary at last, with a haversack on her back . . . She had been to see Kenneth's mother at Seafield, though even allowing for Leza's inexhaustible supply of hospitality she had been away a very long time. Perhaps Mimie had called her in for a cup of tea. The sun had slid west. Yes, I too, must soon away home.

Thank you, God, I said. Thank you, my Saviour. Thank you, Holy Spirit. Thank you for everything: the past, the present and the future.

The Trinity
Protecting me
The Father be
Over me
The Saviour be
Under me
The Spirit be
About me
The Holy Three
Defending me
As evening come
Bless my home
Holy Three
Watching me
As shadows fall
Hear my call
Sacred Three
Encircle me
So it may be
Amen to Thee
Holy Three
About me[2]

14 Blessings

The train squealed to a stop. I had returned to Devon from Fetlar on the same day that Sister Columba and I had arrived exactly seven years previously. It was 21st October, and St Hilarion's day. Stepping out of the train I found that I was being hailed at once by our chaplain. Waving, he hastened towards me, took my case and carried it to his awaiting car.

'Thank you so much for your postcard,' he said as we each fastened our seat belt. 'Coincidentally,' he went on, 'it was identical to the one that Sandy Cheyne sent us last year, when he and his wife and son were on Fetlar.'

'Sandy Cheyne!' I replied in astonishment. 'You mean that the Cheynes who are friends of yours are the same Cheynes who are landowners on Fetlar?'

'Yes,' he said as we pulled out into the road. 'They are relatives by marriage to my wife. I understand that they holiday for a fortnight or so of each summer up there.'

'Yes,' I murmured, my mind spinning round . . . What a fluke this was. 'Yes,' I said again, 'I understand they do.'

Once back at the convent, I decided to say nothing of the decision I had made whilst away, at least not until I had first discussed it with our Warden who was due to pay his quarterly visit at some point during the following month. I knew that the waiting would be a strain, but thought it best. However, November came and went and no word or sign of the Warden did we either hear or see.

'Is Father coming?' one of the Sisters asked Mother one day.

'I'm not sure,' she replied, 'and since we haven't heard at this juncture, I think we must postpone his visit until January . . . I need to write.'

Dismayed by this piece of information, I was spurred at once into action and at the first possible opportunity, sat down to write:

'Dear Father,' I wrote,
'I wanted to see you during your visit to talk to you about a decision I have had to make, but now, since your visit is less imminent than we thought, I thought it best to put it into black and white. I realise that I am either very courageous or completely mad, but have noticed that either way, God doesn't seem to mind so long as we do what we believe (and I most firmly do) is His Will.

I have said nothing of this to Mother as I wanted to talk to you first, but since I can't, I shall give her this letter and its enclosure to read before it is posted on to you.

Please spare me if possible more strain than I already bear. One cannot live with a group of people for more than twenty-one years and not feel it, but I believe absolutely that this is what God wants of me.
Yours very sincerely . . .'

Enclosed with this letter was an outline, though an inadequate one, of my reasonings, and of what I envisaged. My pen scratched away, trying to get the salient points down.

I told how, seven years previously, I had been invited to Iona, and how, during that time, a time that was drastically to change my life, I had felt that God was suggesting that I should take the religious life back to the Isles. I enlarged upon how this call of God was confirmed in a way that made me feel reasonably sure that it was not just simply a case of wishful thinking. Of how for the next seven years I had procrastinated, and that those years had been the most unhappy ones of my life. 'On seven years to the day', I explained, 'I had arrived on

Fetlar, having journeyed to Shetland on the *St Clair*. Interestingly enough I have St Clare for my patron this year, and have been reviving my acquaintance with, and my admiration for her and her ideals,' I wrote, and then continued:

'On my first day on Fetlar, it was a Sunday and because there was no church service, my friends took me up to Halliara-Kirk, a ruined chapel on the hill behind their cottage; and there, we said the Collect, Epistle and Gospel for that particular Sunday. Then, to my surprise, I found myself saying to them that I would like to bring the religious life back to the Isles. God then made it clear to me' – I wrote quickly now – 'during the course of my time on Fetlar that this was what He wanted, and I quailed at the incredibility of even the thought and would have preferred to go on procrastinating and taking the easiest way out, but it was made so vividly clear that I knew without any doubt that it was a case of, "Do it or die". I knew that I had to do what God asked, or else that would be the end of His asking and the end of my vocation as it was meant to be; and only in the knowing of this, and at this point, have I the moral courage to make and pursue this decision, and I request to do so, believing it to be the truth, and asking the Community's blessing.'

Putting down the pen, I stood and collected together my papers. That was as much as there was time for today. Tomorrow I would finish it.

The next afternoon after lunch I fervently went on, to tell in detail of the confirmation of God's call, and how later I had pondered on the hows and whys and wheres of it all. I explained that the answer had come to me in the form of those 'little groups' that a wise elderly priest friend had preached about when I made my simple vows. He had said that the era of large communities was coming to an end and that the future one would be one of 'little flocks'. I envisaged then, I told our Warden, such a group as this, of three or four sisters, living together in a small croft house, as simply as possible; living the Gospel and following as closely as they could the ideals of the early Franciscans, adapting their Rule to mould in with the life on the island, and teaching by their example the values of work and prayer. Their livings would be earned preferably through manual labour, though, where possible, they would give their services freely within the general community. I stopped, and mused, then added that I thought that Rosemary might join me.

'There are a great many disused croft houses going to ruin because of the amalgamation of land,' I told him, 'and this is a fact which is causing great sadness amongst the people. There is one house in particular, at The Ness, which has not long been vacated . . .'

Nearly finished now, I thought. Oh yes . . . I took up my pen again.

'Our chaplain told me on my return, that the Cheyne family, landlords in Fetlar, are good friends of theirs and relatives by marriage to his wife.'

I read through my two missives and folded them up. That night, the eve of the Feast of the Presentation of Our Lady, I gave them to the Reverend Mother asking her to read and forward them to our Warden.

Within a fortnight, two weeks in which I experienced the most cruel anguish of my life and yet out of which came the most exquisite joy, I was free, and privileged indeed to test my call.

It was decided, in order that the call could be tested, that I should be released from my obligations to the Community, though not from my religious vows; for the Community, small in number, did not wish to establish a new house. On the Feast of the Immaculate Conception

119

of Our Lady, the 8th December 1983, for the third time, and at the age of forty-two, I knelt before the altar to state my desire.

On this occasion only three others beside myself were present: The Reverend Mother stood at my side, the Bishop before me, and to the Bishop's left, our Warden.

> 'Blessed is the man who puts his trust in the Lord: he is like a tree planted by the waterside, and never ceases to bear fruit.'

The Warden's voice reverberated around the vacant seats and stalls of the chapel.

> 'Hear the words of St. Paul.
> Rejoice in the Lord always and again I say rejoice. Let your moderation be known to all men. The Lord is at hand. Be careful for nothing; but in everything by prayer and supplication with thanksgiving let your requests be made known unto God. And the peace of God which passes all understanding, shall keep your hearts and minds through Christ Jesus.
> This is the word of the Lord.'

The Warden stopped, and we responded with our 'Thanks be to God,' whilst the Bishop moved a step nearer to the desk where I knelt and proceeded to say the Collect:

> 'Almighty and everlasting God, By whose spirit the whole body of the Church is governed and sanctified: Hear our prayer which we offer for all your faithful people; That each in his vocation and ministry may serve you in holiness and truth to the Glory of your name; Through our Lord and Saviour Jesus Christ.'

The Collect said, the Bishop turned, placed his service sheet in the hands of the Warden, turned back and looked down upon me, and in the tone of powerful authority asked me:

'My daughter, what is your desire?'

I, firm and resolute, answered, 'Remaining in my vows made to God, I desire separation from membership and cessation of obligations to this Community.'

The Bishop stated the act of release, and I returned to him the possessions of the Order: a copy of the Rule, and the ring given me at my profession. He then placed upon my finger another ring, my mother's, as a sign of my continuing consecration and espousal to our Lord Jesus Christ. A short and excellent sermon was preached, and when it was ended the Warden took up once more the threads of the service.

'I remind you all of the words, of our Savour: "Seek ye first the Kingdom of God and his righteousness; and all these things shall be added unto you. Take therefore no thought for the morrow: for the morrow shall take thought for the things of itself. Sufficient unto the day is the evil thereof." '

The Bishop placed his hands upon my head and blessed me with great tenderness, sending me forth with the blessings of Grace, Wisdom and Courage. I stood, and again he said, 'Bless you, Sister,' this time taking my hands, and when released I smiled, genuflected at the altar, and turning, followed the Reverend Mother out of the chapel.

Shortly afterwards I divested myself of the habit of a Community no longer mine. I felt naked; though once dressed in the clothes that had been provided – a pair of trousers, an army surplus shirt, an anorak, and a scarf to tie around my cropped head – I felt that spirit of joy well up inside, and never more like St Francis. God was allowing me this tremendous privilege. He was holding out His hand . . . I took it firmly, and clad thus, I went forth.

*During the warm September of 1985, seventeen months after
my arrival on Fetlar, I was blessed by a pastoral visit from the
Primus of the Episcopal Church in Scotland, the Most Reverend
Alastair Haggart; with him was his wife Mary.*

*The morning after their arrival the Bishop said Mass in the
little oratory of Jesus the Good Shepherd. The three of us knelt,
as the birds awoke and added their own praises to the glory of
God; God the Most Holy Trinity, the Three in One and One in
Three. The sun rose, filling the tiny sanctuary with light. The
Mass was the Mass of the Stigmata of St Francis.*

Standing, the Bishop opened the pages of the missal:

*But God forbid that I should glory, save in the cross of our
Lord Jesus Christ: by whom the world is crucified unto me,
and I unto the world.*

*I cried unto the Lord with my voice: yea, even unto the Lord
did I make my supplication . . .*

15 Miracles

Rosemary, the year after our holiday in Iona, had gone off for several months to nurse her elderly and dying father. After his death, instead of returning to the Community she had accepted a job offered to her in London; and for the final two years before her retirement had lived in Southwark. Thoughts of retirement, though, drew her heart back to Devon; and she bought a small house in Ilfracombe where she settled happily, she thought for the rest of her life, with her little dog Tik.

She was waiting for me that day on Barnstaple station, now seven years older. She raked the platform with her eyes, and to my surprise, although I waved, totally ignored me. Waving again, I realised that she could not have been expecting me to arrive in secular dress. Later, she admitted that never in her life had she been so dumbfounded as when 'this boyish figure' greeted her saying, 'It's all right, I'm still a sister.' Only a few weeks before, on her sixtieth birthday, she had made a great decision, which was, quite definitely and simply, to settle down and accept the fact that she was growing old. This bombshell of an arrival shattered her illusion.

I spent four months with Rosemary in Ilfracombe, making my preparations for the new life ahead. The first thing to do, I decided, was to write to Mr Cheyne. The chaplain had given me his address and I very much felt that since my last call had come in Shetland, that was the place where I must begin. 'Have you any property on Fetlar that you would be willing to lease?' I asked. By the beginning of January I had his reply. The only property that was available, he told me, was The Ness. Precisely the house I wanted.

Rosemary suddenly came to, becoming as excited about the whole venture as I, and on the following day returned from a shopping expedition, pink in the face, and telling me I must come at once.

Busy hemming along the seam of a new habit, I looked up. 'Whatever for?' I asked.

'Because I've seen a marvellous bench table with two benches in a second-hand furniture shop window,' she enthused. 'They're only £20 and exactly right for a little croft house . . . Here's your coat . . . Come along, do . . .' She was in great earnest and terribly afraid someone else might snap them up in our absence.

The table and benches were my first purchase for The Ness; after that, other bits of furniture were rapidly bought. They were polished, painted and mended, and Rosemary's cottage in Ilfracombe soon began to look like a second hand furniture shop too. The Community had given me some money to start off with, and now with half of it – £150 – I had furnished very simply, which is what I wanted, the house in Shetland.

'Well, that's the house and furniture accounted for,' I said with some satisfaction one day. 'The only problem now is, how to get the furniture to the house.'

Several friends suggested that I hire a rent-a-van, and offered very kindly to drive it north for me. Five of this noble contingent were clergy and it was going to be difficult to choose between them, if ever the money could be raised.

'We need a miracle to happen,' I murmured to Rosemary as we pored over an estimate or two from rent-a-van firms. The cheapest rate to hire such a vehicle, to Shetland, was £1600, and all I had was £120!

From time to time a wave of fear swept over me; and one night, drenched by a large one, I got down on to my knees and prayed. If God really wanted me to go ahead, and He was ready to provide the wherewithal with which I could do so, then I on my part was ready to march forward whatever the cost, and nothing – nothing –

would stand in my way. I only wanted, I told Him, what I needed and no more.

The next morning, which happened to be the Feast of St Agnes (21st January), I received two very unexpected cheques through the post; one for £49 and one for £50. Later in the day another envelope was pushed, by hand this time, through the letter box of Rosemary's door, and fell on the mat. We were out at the time and upon our return discovered that it was addressed to me. 'Dear Sister Agnes,' said an enclosed note, 'I thought that you could be doing with this.' The letter was unsigned, and folded neatly into it were ten £10 notes. We were quite overcome, and do not know for certain, to this day, who could have sent it.

I had not received £1600, yet I knew that from then onwards I need have no fears. Indeed, soon afterwards, I received another cheque, this time for £1000, from a clergyman friend of ours in Somerset. Such benevolence, indeed faith, I had never before met and shall never cease to be grateful, for the generosity of that wonderful friend.

Now, only a few hundred pounds short of the rent-a-van target, I accepted an invitation to spend a week with my sister and her husband and three daughters in Worksop. It was likely that after this I would not see them for a very long time, so I felt that the opportunity should not be missed. As it turned out, this visit, in its way, was providential.

Rosemary had persuaded me, rather against my will, whilst I was with Carole to go to Leicester and see and talk to a friend of hers, a Cowley Father. I did not want at that stage really to talk to anyone, though to please her, I agreed.

Carole met me off the coach in Worksop and took me excitedly to her home. After a little refreshment upon our arrival, she said, '. . . and you can take those clothes straight off!' I looked up, slightly surprised and very amused by her adamance, 'I'm not introducing you to my friends', she explained, 'looking like that.'

Apart from a bottle-green duffle coat that Rosemary had lent me, and a red jumper I had bought at a jumble sale in Ilfracombe, I had been wearing the garments that I had left the convent in.

'What's wrong with them?' I asked.

'Baggy trousers,' was all she could say.

In her room she threw open drawers and cupboards, snatched garments from here and there, and re-clothed me from her wardrobe.

Later, whilst she trimmed my hair, we chatted, and she told me among other things how much her Anglican priest at Worksop Priory, a Canon Peter Boulton, was looking forward to meeting me. 'He's suggested you call around and see him,' she said.

'Oh Carole, I don't want to spend my time talking to people – not just yet.'

She looked crestfallen.

'All right,' I said. 'I'll go.'

Sitting in Canon Boulton's office deep in conversation I was glad that I had made the effort, for he was a very nice man. He told me that he knew the Bishop of Exeter well, and was pleased that I had been shown so much kindness by him. He spoke also of various religious communities known to me, including Cowley.

'Actually, I'm going to St John's House in Leicester tomorrow,' I divulged.

A look of pleasure came over his face, 'If you're going to Leicester, why don't you make an appointment to see the Bishop of Leicester too?'

'No, Father,' I jerked out, horrified at the idea. 'There's no reason for me to do that.'

'Yes there is,' he insisted, 'for the Bishop of Leicester is the Chairman of the Advisory Council of Religious Communities, and it would be an excellent thing for him to know about you from the very word go. He's a good friend of mine; shall I give him a ring?'

I was fearful, though he was so matter of fact and reassuring that I allowed him to do so.

It turned out, thankfully, that the Bishop could not see me that day, but coincidentally that he and his wife knew, and had stayed, with the Anglican priest in Shetland who later was to become my spiritual director. A new link had been forged.

Returning to Ilfracombe refreshed from the break, I made my first job a visit to some mutual friends of Rosemary and me. They had very kindly been storing furniture for me in their garage and I wanted to thank them.

'Come in,' said Mary, 'and when we've had a cup of tea Jack will take you up to the garage to see the rest of your furniture. Derek delivered a few more bits and pieces yesterday.'

'Oh yes,' said Jack casually as we drank our tea, 'Derek was asking who was taking the furniture up to Shetland for you. I told him that I thought you were hoping to hire a rent-a-van. He said something about delivering to Shetland himself.'

I choked, put down my cup, and within an hour stood in Derek's shop. His wife Alison actually managed their second hand furniture shop, whilst he ran a furniture removal business alongside it. They were both there when I breathlessly arrived.

'Do you really deliver up to Shetland, Derek?' I asked.

'No,' he replied. 'Though I've always wanted to go to Shetland, and I'll move every stone I can to do it as cheaply as possible for you if you'll allow me to have the job.'

I said that I would be delighted to give him the job if I could manage the price, and the next morning he arrived at Rosemary's door with an estimate in his hand.

'Having made numerous telephone calls,' he told us, 'I find that the cheapest way we can do it is this . . .'

What he suggested astounded us.

'I will get the older of my two furniture vans MOT-ed and take your stuff to Shetland in that. Then, to make the trip cheaper, what I plan to do is to leave it on Fetlar with you . . .'

We gaped.

'How does that work?' said Rosemary.

He laughed. 'I was going to sell it anyway, you see, and I won't get more than two or three hundred pounds for it . . . so if you have it, you'll see something for your money, and we'll have had the pleasure of a lovely trip.'

By that stage we had all hoped Alison his wife would go off on the adventure with him.

'You mean you'll save several hundred pounds on not having to bring an empty van of that size all the way back from Shetland to Devon?' I quavered. He nodded. 'How much then is your final estimate?'

'£1,200,' he said, looking boyishly pleased.

I looked at Rosemary, and then back to Derek, and put out my hand to shake his. 'That's exactly what I've got,' I told him.

Later, in Shetland, I sold the truck, and what I got for it supported me for my first six months.

Living by faith with no regular income, and sometimes no income at all, means that I cannot afford, on the whole, to have jobs done for me. Therefore one has to do them oneself, or depend upon the charity of friends.

The first major job, after my arrival at The Ness, was re-roofing the byre, the workshop and the barn. Deciding to start with the barn I saved up for several months for a drum of tar. After that, some settled weather had to be waited for, and when at last the perfect week came I made a splendid start. By the end of the third day I had almost completed the job. Rotten boards had been replaced, new felt patches tacked on top, and then strip by strip I had tarred, covered the roof with hessian, and then tarred again. 'Nearly there,' I murmured, standing back to admire my handiwork. 'I only need to get this last strip sealed today and it will save me from reopening the drum and getting stuck up with tar again tomorrow.'

I peered through the but room window. It was twenty past four by the clock; time, alas, that I began to clear up. I walked back to the barn; it was beginning to mizzle. Skerry and Flugga, who were then kittens, yet who already knew my timetable better than I knew it myself, danced after and before me, drawing my attention to the fact that it was time for their tea. Mine was at 5.30 p.m., and Vespers followed. Yes, I ought really to stop. It was Trinitytide, the season often referred to by one of our clergy friends as the 'greenbelt'. My beautiful green belt of grass around the barn was spattered with spots of black tar. It would take me another half hour to finish, I reckoned, weighing up the amount of work still to be done. Yes, I decided, I would forge ahead. The Lord, surely, would understand my reasonings.

Moving the ladder I had borrowed from Kenny, I laid it up against the skew at the end of the roof. I picked up my newly filled bucket of tar in one hand and a brush in the other, and made my last ascent. There was going to be just enough tar to finish the job; that was good. Lodging the bucket and brush against the ladder, I snicked a piece out of the hessian to make it sit a little more comfortably. Then, having unstuck my fingers from the glued-up scissors, I again picked up the brush and bucket. Oozing the tar in behind the join, I patted it down.

This last bit was going to be a fiddle I could see . . . and more likely to take three-quarters of an hour. Now let me think . . .

Whoosh! the ladder slipped on the newly wet grass. The bucket went up, and its contents came down over me and we all landed in a crumpled heap upon the ground. Untangling myself and a rather buckled bucket from the ladder – I couldn't see the brush – I noticed that my right wrist was alarmingly swollen.

What a fool I was, and especially to have wasted so much tar; that was the worrying thing. I looked at the drum and wondered if enough could be scraped out to finish the job. Not today, though, for I had learned a very salutary lesson. Never again must my rule be broken; excepting of course for some urgent reason or for the sake of charity. Now, what about my wrist? Was that broken too? It'll have to wait, I decided, looking at it, and again at the mess. And I simply couldn't walk over to the nurse's house looking like a tar-baby. The kittens mewed pitifully, frantic now for their tea, whilst I, in a somewhat restricted way, waved my arms and told them to wait. If only Mimie would pay me one of her welcome calls; she would put the kettle on for hot water . . . How on earth does one get tar off in this quantity anyhow? Oh dear, it was already beginning to set. I must hurry.

Three hours later, exhausted, red in the face, sore and very thoughtful, I sat at the bench table in front of a belated tea. I poured out my first cup. Was that a click? Yes, the garden gate. I listened . . . Footsteps.

'Come in, Mimie,' I said. 'You're just in time for a cup of tea.'

16 Home

I walked into the church wearing for the first time the new habit I had made, and feeling completely happy and at home in it. It had been sewn entirely by hand, was oatmeal in colour, cut quite simply in the shape of a cross, and had a large blue Celtic cross stitched on the front. Over a white wimple and headband I wore a veil as blue as the bluest sea, and on my feet, sandals.

Sunlight filtered in through the stained glass windows and danced a rainbow of colours down the aisle before me. At the high altar a priest stood waiting, his arms outspread in welcome. I walked towards him, knelt on the altar step and he laid his hands upon my head. The church was decorated with Easter flowers and the air scented with spring, and with the sweet aroma of a new beginning.

'In the name of the Father and of the Son and of the Holy Ghost . . .' he began.

In the choir stalls, slightly behind me and down either side, sat twelve of my closest friends. Birds twittered in the treetops outside, and the Reverend Prebendary Arthur Chandler, who had been so great a friend and priestly counsellor during my sojourn in Ilfracombe, continued. First he blessed the new habit, and then myself with the words:

'Unto God's most gracious mercy and protection we commend you. May He keep you ever close to Himself, that you may find in His love your strength and peace: May He give you the true courage which shows itself by gentleness, the true wisdom which shows itself by simplicity; true power which shows itself by modesty. May He guard you from stumbling, and set you before the presence of His glory without blemish in exceeding joy.

'Go forth unto the Isles in peace. Be of good courage: uphold that which is good. Strengthen the faint-hearted, support the weak, help the afflicted. Love and serve the Lord, rejoicing in the power of the Holy Spirit. And may the blessing of God Almighty, the Father, the Son and the Holy Ghost be with you now and forever.   Amen.'

It was the 22nd April 1984 and Easter Day, a day when in the parish church of Holy Trinity, Ilfracombe my joy was as resplendent as the day itself. The sun blazed down out of a cloudless sky and we were a merry gathering: Rosemary, Jack and Mary, Alison and Derek, Margaret, Violet, Joyce, another Margaret, Father Chandler and his wife, and me. Rosemary produced a lovely celebratory tea and afterwards when our friends had all gone, she and I walked, on that perfect evening, around a local park.

Two days later we waved farewell to a very excited Alison and Derek as they pulled out from Horne Road in the furniture van, to begin their long journey to Fetlar.

'Goodbye,' we shouted. 'See you in Aberdeen on Friday . . . Goodbye . . . Good lodgings.'

We ourselves set off the next day by train. After breakfast, our bags packed, Tikki groomed and looking perkily excited too about the adventure, we waited for Father Chandler to pick us up. He had kindly offered to drive us to the station. As we waited, the post arrived with just one letter for me. I opened it as Rosemary called out to tell me that Father had arrived. It was from the Bishop of Exeter, sending me his final blessing and wishing me well.

By the Friday evening of that same week we were reunited with Alison and Derek, who awaited us at the P & O ferry terminal in Aberdeen. What fun it all was! We were intoxicated by the excitement of launching out into the deep; all of us, that is, excepting Rosemary. She seemed slightly subdued, though she assured me forcefully that she was having a lovely time.

At the reception desk we waited for our tickets and boarding cards. How courteous and welcoming the P & O staff are, I thought, but my thoughts were interrupted by a gruff voice addressing me from behind. 'Excuse me, Sister, are you on the way to Fetlar?'

I spun round to find an upright, elderly man, Jim Jamieson, who was later to become our very good friend. 'Yes,' I said, 'I am.'

'I'm a Fetlar man,' he enlightened me, and put out his hand. 'Welcome to Fetlar.'

The *St Clair* pulled out from the quay at 6 p.m. and the four of us stood silently on deck and watched Aberdeen slip quietly away into oblivion. Truly, I felt, I was homeward bound.

I had been closely in touch with the Church in the north, mostly in the person of the Reverend Lewis Shand Smith, who is the Rector of Lerwick and the only Anglican priest ministering in Shetland. Both he and the Bishop of Aberdeen and Orkney, whose diocese I would be in, had offered their advice, prayers and blessing.

God works in many wonderful and mysterious ways, I mused; and what new friends and adventures now, would this glorious beginning hold?

We arrived on Fetlar at 11.15 a.m. the following day. Mr Jamieson had kindly offered to drive Rosemary, Tikki and me from the ferry terminal in Lerwick to Fetlar by car, for there was not, we found, room for all of us in the furniture van. It was cold and wet, and at a later date Rosemary laughingly confessed that she had not wanted to come to the ends of the world with me one little bit. Apart, she said, from feeling the need to see me settled in. The mist swirled around, the visibility was almost nil, and my hopes that her first impression would be a glowing one, fast disappeared. 'No, I wasn't a bit impressed,' she told me, 'and continually expected to see a viking ship loom out of the gloom.'

Mr Jamieson dropped us at the home of Kenny, Mimie and Anne, and there we found a heart-warming welcome. Not only had they The Ness key ready for us to collect, but also a meal prepared and waiting for us four hungry travellers to eat. I was looking forward, though, to pressing on to The Ness, and to seeing it now with the knowledge that it was home. Very gratefully, yet with great restraint, I ate my meal. Everyone else chatted, frustratingly indifferent and in a completely unhurried and relaxed sort of way. However, although it seemed much longer, only an hour had elapsed before we duly arrived, and it was to find the house sparklingly clean and welcoming with pots of daffodils in each of its windows. Our friend Anne had evidently spent many hours getting it ready.

The six of us, for Mimie had stayed at home, unloaded the van surprisingly quickly. Then, bidding goodbye for the moment to Kenny and Anne, we found that the mist had lifted and the sun had come out.

Alison and Derek had to leave us the following morning, so we hoped that they would make the most of their time.

'Why not go off for a walk?' we suggested. 'Down to the beach or along the banks?'

They jumped at the chance, and as soon as they had departed, we set earnestly to work. There was a lot of organising and rearranging to be done in those seven little rooms. We erected beds, made them up, laid down mats, and found enough crockery and cutlery to set the table. We located a kettle and a teapot and enough food to make a simple tea. They were astonished when they returned to find a cosy meal by the fire, in a tidy house that already felt like home.

Rosemary stayed on in Shetland for about six weeks,

helping me to settle in. We emulsioned walls, stained floors, painted, and pulled the garden into shape. Being the end of April meant that it was time for the maincrop seed, too, to be sown, if indeed it was possible to sow. I had looked blearily out of the windows at the rough grassy area at the back of the house on the day we arrived. It would take months, I had chewed over, to dig it by hand, for it had long been a field. Nevertheless, one afternoon during our first few days I was busily occupied weeding the small walled garden at the front, when a noise interrupted my ploys. The rattling sound of a car drew nearer until at last a vehicle eventually appeared and snorted around the corner to a halt. A door was flung open, and a young man with two dogs jumped out. The man at once strode over.

'I'm Andrew Hughson,' he said, holding out a hand. 'My wife Sheila and I croft the land around your house.' He shook my hand vigorously, 'We heard you were coming. You're making a fine job there I see . . . are you going to cultivate the land at the back of the house too?'

I said that I was hoping to grow vegetables there. 'Except . . .'

'It needs going over with a plough,' he said, rubbing his chin. 'Tell you what, I'm bringing a tractor down here next week to do my own tattie field, the one over there,' he said, pointing north-east. 'I'll run over your bit too if you like?'

I was astounded, and due to this tremendous kindness was able, in quite good time, to get all the spring sowing done, though I had to spend many hours every day banging down the ridges with a rake to get enough fine tilth. However, that summer produced a plethora of potatoes, carrots and onions; enough in fact to take myself and any visitors who came to stay, the whole cycle round to the following year's crops. Also, I grew a splendid amount of the seasonal peas, beans, radishes, lettuces and beets. Now, of course, being a great deal more organised, there is enough and to spare to give or to sell. On one occasion a gentleman from the Crofters' Commission happened to be on Fetlar with his colleagues and surprised me by knocking at my door and asking if he might take a photograph of the garden. My crops were particularly good that year and they had apparently impressed him.

'I've never seen anything like it in Shetland,' he told me, though I felt sure he had.

Although this is a very remote little island, an unusual number of people find their way to my door. Within two consecutive days of one summer I had as many as twenty unexpected visitors. This particular avalanche started one sunny morning whilst I was operating a primitive printing press I had given a home to. The work that day had not gone well, my hands were inky and my face smudged. Someone called out. Who on earth could it be, I wondered, and stepped through the workshop door to see. A lady was peering in through the byre.

'Are you Sister Agnes?' she inquired as I appeared, and she might well have asked.

Offering her, her husband and four daughters a cup of tea, I heard the sound of a car. We waited, and soon Bob the postman swung round in his van. Handing me the mail, he beamed.

'There's another car load looking for you at the top of the road,' he chuckled; and so the day went on.

At the end of it, tired and behind schedule and ravenously hungry, though I had had umpteen cups of tea, I prepared my supper. Just as I neared the point of actually carrying it through to the but room, the sound of yet another car was again to be heard. I switched off the oven and opened the door. To my delighted surprise I found that this time it was a young man from Devon, whose two elderly aunts I had known.

'They'd kill me,' he smiled, stooping in through the porch and accompanied by an ornithologist friend, 'if I'd

136

been to Fetlar and hadn't been in to see you.'

'You're very welcome,' I assured them. 'Have you had supper?'

Later, as we sat by the fire, they told me that they were on Fetlar looking mostly for the storm petrel.

'Actually,' said Andrew, 'it was rather ridiculous. We met a group of bird watchers yesterday who told us with great excitement that they had been to Fetlar. They had seen some very rare birds; "and," they said, "we saw the nun." So we knew you were here.'

I laughed. Their story made me feel very much at home. 'I see,' I murmured. 'So I fall into the same category as the snowy owl.'

Rosemary returned to Shetland in the autumn of my first year and could hardly wait to get back. Although the first journey up had been made with grave reservations, within a fortnight of that particular arrival she had begun, to her surprise, though not to mine, to negotiate the buying of Lower Ness. Much earlier in Devon, before she had known anything of my venture, she had firmly resolved to give up all idea of becoming a sister. Later, after deep consideration about joining me, she decided finally that she did not want to land me, she said, 'with a geriatric'. She did, however, feel very drawn to living alongside the hoped-for little group and providing hospitality for the many folk already wanting to come and stay. So, although she had not joined me in the sense of becoming a sister, she bought Lower Ness and gave new life to a croft house that would otherwise have been doomed.

Now, living on the Ness point only a few hundred yards away, she permanently supports me in every aspect of my religious life; coming to Terce and Vespers and Compline each day; joining me in intercessions and private prayer; sharing the labours of the land; helping me in the offering of hospitality and acting often as a go-between and representative of myself, both here on

Fetlar and further afield. I owe her heartfelt thanks and am blessed indeed to have so faithful and stalwart a friend.

Life is full, lived within its simple framework. Full, of the rigours and hardships that come with being human, and of having to make a living. Though full also, of that joy which is interwoven in the love of God.

I always knew that the byre would convert into a lovely chapel; and now that the oratory was becoming too small for the amount of visitors wishing to join us at prayer, I had made a start.

It had been raining heavily and, unable to work in the garden as I had planned that day, I pondered upon what could be done, and began. Rosemary down at Lower Ness heard the first hammerings and decided to lie low!

First on the agenda, I decided, must be the cattle stalls which ran stoutly up the centre of the building. I yanked three of them out. That took ages, yet was well worth doing for now we had space, and the wood salvaged made into rough though adequate

138

pews. I banged in several more nails and smiled. My friend Aileen, who is a crofter's wife, had told me how fed-up her husband Alex gets if she bullies him long enough into doing certain jobs. 'You should be a nun,' he now tells her, 'then you could do them yourself.'

I picked up the hammer; a new door would have to be made. Looking round on a later occasion, I felt pleased. Those two roof supports, which had so exercised my mind, and which were very necessary, had blended in well; one to become a huge cross rising up from the altar, and the second, the lectern.

I knelt in a cloud of dust. I hoped that one day when the conversion was finished we would be able to have this chapel dedicated to the Holy Cross and the Mother of Him who hung thereon. Strangely, after deciding upon this for a dedication I found that one of the major church sites on Fetlar had been that of a 'Cross-kirk'. Appropriately too, the second-hand caravan I have just been able to buy through a second wonderful donation from our kind priest benefactor in Somerset, arrived on the Feast of Our Lady of Sorrows. It stands alongside one of the walls of the chapel and one day we hope to encase it. It is to be called The Anchorhold, or Our Lady's Anchor.

I put down my tools and stood up. Flugga padded in, and giving me no more than a fleeting glance jumped on to a pew. I walked over and sat beside him, knowing only too well his true intentions, though perhaps we would have peace for a while.

I looked around once more. There was still much to be done, both manually here and to be built into the future. How? I did not know, nor did I need to worry. All of it lay in the Providence and safe keeping of God. We needed only to take each day as it came.

Flugga placed a paw on my lap, his first strategical move, I knew, towards tea. I ignored it.

One entered the religious life because one believed oneself to have heard a particular call to leave all, and follow our Lord

Jesus Christ. Walking in the way of the Evangelical Counsels, I had been taught. That was true, and yet there were many calls and many different kinds of vocation. One could be called to be a doctor, a nurse, a teacher, a butcher, a baker, a candlestick maker, or just an ordinary housewife. Anything, and not one call was greater than the other, for the greatest call for any of us is the one which is peculiar to us, and for which God has prepared us.

A great friend of the Community to which I belonged, a priest, once said that the greatest contemplative he ever knew was a little Scots housewife who lived in the back streets of Glasgow, because all she did, she did for the glory of God. This then is what 'vocation' is all about. It doesn't matter what we do, or how mundane it may be . . . whether it's sweeping the floor, or washing the dishes, answering letters (and letter writing for me could become a mission in itself), or digging in the garden, so long as we do it for the glory of God.

Flugga had eased his whole self on to my knee and stared magnetically at me.

'You shall have your meal soon, Flugga,' I told him.

I hope amongst so many hopes that what is being built up in this place will become generally known as the Society of Our Lady of the Isles, SOLI – and what a variety of meanings even its abbreviated form has!

Will God send other women to join me, I wondered. Like-minded souls, who wish to give themselves wholly to Him within the religious life. Or, does He mean me to continue to develop a solitary vocation?

I had never lived alone until I came to Fetlar, and how apprehensive I had been. Yet, what blessings it has brought and how many new dimensions it has opened up. No, I need not worry. The house itself has a lovely, happy feel, and I have in the heart of it our Lord's presence in the most blessed Sacrament of the altar.

Then there are too, of course, my two little cats, the dearest of friends to me, and a whole island of people whom I have grown to think of affectionately as extended family. Three years I have

141

been here, a good three years in every way. I have given God everything and everything has been given back in abundance. I had nothing and everything has been provided.

No, it is not so much what we 'do' or try to do that is important, but what we are. 'Being' rather than 'doing' comes first, for what we do comes out of what we are.

The chapel door lay open. The air was warm and fragrant and Christ's words came to my mind:

> Consider the lilies how they grow: they toil not, they spin not; and yet I say unto you, that Solomon in all his glory was not arrayed like one of these. If then God so clothe the grass which is today in the field, and tomorrow is cast into the oven; how much more will he clothe you, O ye of little faith? And seek not ye what ye shall eat, or what ye shall drink, neither be ye of doubtful mind. For all these things do the nations of the world seek after: and your Father knoweth that ye have need of these things. But rather seek ye the kingdom of God; and all these things shall be added unto you. Fear not, little flock; for it is your Father's good pleasure to give you the kingdom. Sell that ye have, and give alms; provide yourselves bags which wax not old, a treasure in the heavens that faileth not, where no thief approacheth, neither moth corrupteth. For where your treasure is, there will your heart be also.

Where our treasure is, there will our heart be also. One has to give 'everything' to find that treasure. To buy the 'pearl of great price'. It demands the giving of our whole self to God, whatever our calling. It demands that we should stand before Him unprotected, vulnerable, shorn of pretensions, in truth, and desiring not our own will but only His. Then, and only then, will life become that eternal miracle of glory.

Skerry jumped on to my lap to join Flugga. What a load! He stretched out a furry paw and touched my cheek. Rising from my seat, I gently untangled them.

The sunlight streamed in through a skylight and danced on

142

the stonework of the walls. Those skylights would have to be repaired somehow; the wood was soft and pulpy and they leaked like a sieve . . . Flugga rubbed persuasively against the skirts of my habit.

I turned, and with the two of them following, both tails this time triumphantly erect, I went into the house to find them some tea.

Notes

Chapter 1 1	CHILDHOOD *The Divine Office*, Society of St Margaret, East Grinstead, published by Oxford University Press, 1953. Antiphon to the Magnificat, for First Vespers of the Second Sunday in Advent
Chapter 2 1	SCHOOLDAYS *The Divine Office*, Antiphon to Vespers for the First Week in Advent, Monday
Chapter 3 1	NANNY *The English Missal*, W. Knott & Son, 3rd edition, 1958. Collect for the First Mass of Christmas
Chapter 4 1 2	SCOTLAND David Adam, *The Edge of Glory*, Triangle, 1985 G.R.D. McLean, *Poems of the Western Highlanders*, SPCK, 1962. I have adapted the fifth line, which originally reads: 'Sun on the mountains high ashine'
Chapter 5 1 2	SORROW *The Divine Office*, Lauds antiphon to the Benedictus, for the Second Sunday in Epiphany ibid., Little Chapter for the First Vespers of the Feast of the Epiphany
Chapter 6 1	GREENWOODS *The English Missal*, Introit for the Third, Fourth and Fifth Sundays after Epiphany (Psalm 97.1 BCP)
Chapter 8 1	THE CONVENT *The Divine Office*, Prime hymn
Chapter 10 1	A HARBOUR From 'The Voice of the Ocean', tr. Patrick McGlyn in *The Owl Remembers*, an anthology

selected by John McKenzie, Stirling, 1933
2   *The Divine Office*, Collect for First and Second
Vespers of Easter (Collect for Easter Day, BCP)

Chapter 12   THE END OF AN ERA
1   I. Marion McNeill (ed.), *An Iona Anthology*,
The Iona Community

Chapter 13   FETLAR
1   David Adam, *The Edge of Glory*
2   ibid.